SHIPPING
An Introduction to the Technical, Operational and Commercial Aspects

Dedication

This book is dedicated to the people who make shipping work. The people on the ships, the people who work in harbours, docks and shipyards, the pilots, surveyors, maritime lawyers, maritime regulators and all of those who arrange the business of ships and shipping. Most of them never feature in the various awards ceremonies held each year but without them there would be no shipping industry.

Nigel Draffin

SHIPPING
An Introduction to the Technical, Operational and Commercial Aspects

by

Nigel Draffin

M.I.Mar.E.S.T.

First Edition

Foreword by
Peter Hinchliffe OBE
Secretary General
International Chamber of Shipping

Published by
Petrospot Limited
England
2014

Published in the United Kingdom by

Petrospot Limited
Petrospot House, Somerville Court, Trinity Way,
Adderbury, Oxfordshire OX17 3SN, England

www.petrospot.com
Tel: +44 1295 814455
Fax: +44 1295 814466

© Nigel Draffin 2014

First published 2014

British Library Cataloguing in Publication Data

A catalogue record for this book is available from
the British Library

ISBN 978-1-908663-19-1

This publication is designed to provide accurate and authoritative
information in regard to the subject matter covered. It is sold with the
understanding that the publisher is not engaged in rendering legal,
accounting, or other professional service. If legal advice or other expert
assistance is required, the services of a competent professional person
should be sought.

Petrospot books are available at special quantity discounts
for use in corporate training programmes or onboard ships

Petrospot Limited (www.petrospot.com)
Designed by Cheryl Marshall, Petrospot Limited
Printed in the United Kingdom
by Stephens Print Solutions
(www.stephensprintsolutions.com)

Foreword

Shipping is as international, diverse, challenging and complex as any industry could ever be. But it is also uniquely absorbing and rewarding.

The industry is changing very quickly. Ships are getting bigger, ports are getting deeper and the Panama Canal is getting wider. The Northern Sea Route is opening up and trading patterns are changing. As the centre of gravity of the industry continues to shift eastwards, oil and commodity markets have seldom been more volatile, freight rates under more pressure or finance harder to come by. Improvements in technology and communications are coming thick and fast. Sustainability has become the buzzword and requirements on air emissions and ballast water are forcing the pace of change. The fuels are changing too, with liquefied natural gas (LNG), methanol, glycerol and others now vying for attention as distillates mount a challenge on the dominance of heavy fuel oil. The interest in abatement technology is steadily growing.

Against this background, the need for industry knowledge, education and hands on experience has never been greater, both at sea or onshore. In this context, this book by shipping and bunker industry expert Nigel Draffin is a perfect starting place.

Shipping: An Introduction to the Technical, Operational and Commercial Aspects aims to educate and inform newcomers to shipping and those whose jobs require a basic grasp of how the industry works. In that respect it handsomely delivers. The book offers a valuable insight into all aspects of shipping and deserves its place alongside the specialist technical and academic books available elsewhere.

It outlines the types of ships plying the world's oceans and the vast support infrastructure required to service the supply chain and keep the ships moving. It begins by looking at world trade and cargo flows and examines the fundamental properties of ships – why do they float; why do they sink? – before identifying the categories of vessel currently in service. It will be as helpful for the novice as it will be interesting for the more experienced seafarer or shipping professional.

Nigel's book takes the reader through the duties expected of the crew, from watchkeeping to catering, and looks at manning, training, welfare and crew retention. It covers navigation and traffic management systems, communications and onboard safety. There are sections on classification and insurance, international conventions and national maritime law.

Nigel looks at ports and the services they offer, such as pilots and agents, cranes and dry docks. He also examines the many types of craft operating in ports.

Ships exist to make money for the owners and charterers, and the financial aspect of shipping is not ignored. Nigel looks at charter parties and contracts of affreightment, at shipbroking and vessel vetting, and at the main costs, such as manning, maintenance, insurance and bunkering. He covers sale and purchase, new building and scrapping, as well as ownership structures, mortgages and public and private ownership issues.

Ships would sail nowhere without propulsion systems and Nigel excels in describing the engines and propellers, speed and efficiency, and puts into context the issues of greenhouse gases, emissions regulation and pollution.

Piracy and the proliferation of high risk areas are now key issues for crews and ships and are therefore covered. So too are disputes, ship arrest, liens, claim resolution, mediation and arbitration.

Nigel provides a handy 'where to go for help' section and a glossary of abbreviations and shipping terms. The book also includes some helpful appendices to illustrate what might be found in voyage and time charter contracts.

All in all, this is a very accomplished piece of work which I am certain will be a great asset to anyone embarking on a career in international shipping or wanting to know more about different sectors of this great global industry.

I am very grateful to Nigel Draffin for having brought this book to fruition and am delighted to recommend it.

Peter Hinchliffe OBE
Secretary General
International Chamber of Shipping

May 2014

Preface

In early 2013, Llewellyn Bankes-Hughes asked me if I would write a book on shipping – when I asked why, he said that there was a need for a book which explained the basics of ships and shipping for new entrants to the maritime sector and for non-specialists. At first I was unsure that I could contribute anything useful but, as I thought about his suggestion, I realised that most of the existing works on this subject were quite specialised and did not present the 'whole picture' of shipping at an accessible level. I hope that this book will enable people to put all the different parts of the business of ships, cargo and shipping commerce into context and to find the answers to most questions about the industry that are outside their experience.

This is not a high-level academic work nor is it a text book for professional study. It is a book that will hopefully increase understanding for new entrants to the industry and those moving from one sector to another. There will be many omissions and, I am sure, some errors, for which the fault is mine. However, I have been fortunate to have had the help and guidance of a great number of industry professionals and specialists in the production of the text.

If I manage to increase understanding of our industry then I will be content.

Nigel Draffin

May 2014

About the author

Shipping: An Introduction to the Technical, Operational and Commercial Aspects is a much-needed and unique addition to the plethora of specialist books already available on almost every aspect of the global shipping industry. The fact that it has been written by Nigel Draffin, a proven expert many times over in shipping and bunkering, guarantees that it will be comprehensive, accessible to everyone who needs to learn the basics about shipping and also very useful for anyone who, on occasion, may need to check forgotten facts or find a starting point for further research.

This book is Nigel's seventh but the first to look into the diverse and complex world of shipping. His previous six titles all deal with bunkering in some form or other, including liquefied natural gas (LNG) bunkering, ships' engines and commercial issues, but this book sails a new course.

Nigel has been involved in shipping for almost 50 years and with the commercial bunker market for over 25 years. After joining Shell Tankers as an apprentice engineer in 1966, he progressed through the ranks, serving on all classes of vessel, including very large crude carriers (VLCCs) and LNG tankers. He came ashore in 1979 to join the newbuilding department of Shell International Marine. After two years of new construction in Ireland, South Korea and the Netherlands, he transferred to Shell's Research & Development unit, specialising in control systems, fuel combustion and safety systems.

In 1986, Nigel moved to the commercial department as a bunker buyer and economics analyst. In 1988, he was promoted to be Head of Operational Economics, responsible for all of the fuel purchased for the Shell fleet, the operation of the risk management policy and the speed/performance of the owned fleet. In March 1996, he joined the staff of E.A. Gibson Shipbrokers Ltd in the bunker department, and became the manager. In 2006, this department merged with US-based broking house LQM Petroleum Services, where Nigel is currently Senior Broker and Technical Manager.

Nigel is a founder member of the International Bunker Industry Association (IBIA) and has served several times on its council of management and executive board. He has also served as the association's Chairman. He is the author of IBIA's *Basic Bunkering Course* and Director of Petrospot's leading training events, the *Oxford Bunker Course*, the *Oxford Bunker Course (Advanced)*, and *An Introduction to LNG Bunkering*. Nigel is a member of the Institute of Marine Engineering, Science and Technology and Past Master of the Worshipful Company of Fuellers.

Llewellyn Bankes-Hughes
Managing Director, Petrospot Limited

May 2014

Acknowledgements

The author extends his thanks to everyone who has helped in the creation of *Shipping: An Introduction to the Technical, Operational and Commercial Aspects*, particularly Doug Barrow, Steve Christie, Trevor Harrison and David Hughes who suggested many additions and changes which hopefully make the book better. He also extends his thanks to Llewellyn Bankes-Hughes and his team at Petrospot for suggesting the idea in the first place and, in particular, to Lesley Bankes-Hughes and Cheryl Marshall who have seamlessly designed and produced the finished article.

Nigel Draffin

May 2014

Contents

Contents

List of Figures

Introduction

People moved goods on water before 10,000 BC and long before they discovered the wheel (which emerged about 3,500 BC), and waterborne transport continues to provide the most energy efficient and practical way to move goods over distance. Building and using rafts, boats and then ships became a specialised activity with skills and techniques developing in different communities, being adapted and adopted as trade between those communities developed.

As soon as shipping goods and people by water became a collective endeavour, societies developed rules, commercial practices and informal structures to spread the individual and economic risk and reward, and many of the business tools we use today were developed many thousands of years ago.

Maritime insurance has its origins in the trading of Chinese, Babylonian and Rhodian merchants between 3,000 and 2,000 BC. The concept of hiring a vessel and crew to carry goods goes back to the man with a raft and knowledge of the waters and currents of a river who would transport you and your goods across a river for a fee. The codification of laws concerning marine transport developed alongside the ability to write them down and for states to enforce them. They were often based on the practices of trading cities, including the cities of the Hanseatic League, the town of Amalfi and the rolls of Oleron. The rolls were published by Queen Eleanor of Aquitaine in 1160 AD and she introduced them to England.

It is easy to forget that in the period around 500 BC, men had the skill and talent to build vessels capable of a voyage from the eastern Mediterranean to Northern Europe, carrying goods for trade. Some historians claim that by the height of the Roman Empire the trade between that empire and India was over 300,000 tonnes per annum by sea, involving 300 ships using the monsoon winds. It is also no accident that most of the world biggest cities were either seaports or situated on large rivers.

Notes

Throughout this book I have tried to use the units of Système Internationale (SI); this can become complicated because some units are specific to the shipping industry (knots, nautical miles, feet) and there can be confusion with units of mass. I have used tonne throughout although many readers may be familiar with metric ton (mt) – these two are identical and interchangeable. Where ton is used without the prefix 'metric', it will be as a long ton (imperial units, a ton of 2,240 pounds) or a short ton (US units, a ton of 2,000 pounds).

The table below may help.

Nautical mile (NM)	1,852 metres	Distance on the earth's surface (one minute of arc on any meridian)
Knot (kt)	1 nautical mile per hour	Ship speed, wind speed, water speed (current)
Tonne (MT)	1,000 kilogrammes	Also written Metric Ton
TEU	Twenty-foot equivalent unit	Basic size of shipping containers
CEU	Car equivalent unit	Measure for car carriers

A note on what to call the ship!

Various 'style guides' offer different advice over the use of 'ship', 'vessel' and 'boat', and also whether the ship should be referred to as 'she', 'her' or 'it'.

My choice is to use all three terms in order to make the text more user friendly. As an ex-seafarer, I know a ship is always feminine.

Chapter 1 - World trade

In 1950, world seaborne trade was estimated at 0.5 billion tonnes per annum. At the time of writing, it has reached over 9 billion tonnes. This is carried by more than 50,000 ships with a carrying capacity of 1.4 billion metric tonnes (MT). This trade can be split up into cargo types and into some well-defined trade routes. Statistics from a 2013 United Nations Conference on Trade and Development (UNCTAD) report showed that in 2012 seaborne trade accounted for some 85% of total trade. The breakdown of seaborne trade is tankers (33.4%), major dry bulk commodities (iron ore, coal, grain, alumina and bauxite, and phosphate) (28.3%), containers (16.6%) and the remainder as general dry cargo.

In assessing the container trades, UNCTAD has highlighted the fact that whilst the number of vessels in the sector has remained largely static for 10 years, vessel size and container numbers (as twenty-foot equivalent units (TEU)) have increased sharply (by 100%), whilst the number of liner services and the number of participating companies have fallen by about 20%.

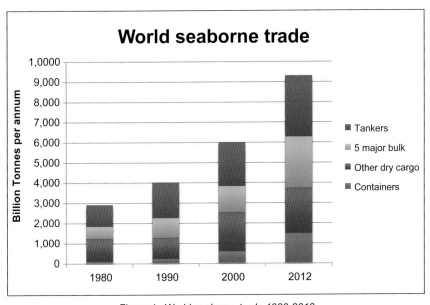

Figure 1. World seaborne trade 1980-2012

Trade routes

Trade routes vary considerably according to the vessel sector and they are influenced by shifts in geographical location of sources of production and consumption. The tanker and major dry bulk sectors are tied to the sources of materials which are largely static. However, their destinations can shift with demand.

The historic trade routes for the main commodities are as follows:

Oil – From the sources in the Mid East Gulf, South East Asia, West Africa, Central and South America and North Europe to the refiners and consumers worldwide. The dominant routes are Mid East to Asia and West Africa to the United States and Europe

Coal – From the sources in Australia, Indonesia, Russia, South America and South Africa to Europe and Asia

Grain – From Europe, Argentina, Australia, Canada and the United States to North Africa, China, India, Japan, Mid East and Thailand

Bauxite and alumina – From Africa, America (North, Central and South) and Australia to Europe, North America and Japan

Phosphate – From Australia, South America, China, Egypt, the Baltic region and Morocco to consumers worldwide.

Container trades are linked to the circulation of the very large vessels that run on defined liner routes and subsidiary networks of feeder vessels that shift containers to and from the major 'hub' ports able to serve the very big vessels. Most vessel operators formed cooperative groups to try to maintain some stability in freight rates and avoid unnecessary duplication of services. Such arrangements were called 'conferences', but they have fallen foul of legislation on competition and have been partly replaced by 'alliances' which endeavour to do the same without falling foul of the law.

The routes for these big vessels are based on round the world trading (East and West directions):

From Far East via Malacca, Suez, Gibraltar, North Europe, US East Coast, Gulf Coast, Panama, California, and then returning to the Far East

Far East, India, South Africa and West Africa returning to the Far East

Far East to the US West Coast returning to the Far East.

The smaller vessels also operate North-South routes between hub ports and smaller ports and cover routes with lower demand.

Some specialist vessels (refrigerated cargo vessels and vehicle carriers) operate on trade routes specific to their cargo.

Trade routes by vessel density

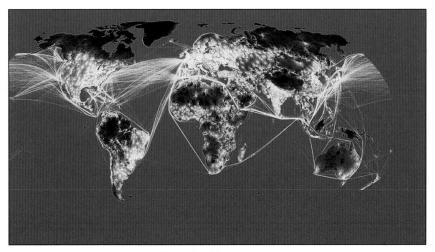

Figure 2. Shipping routes

Trade route matrix

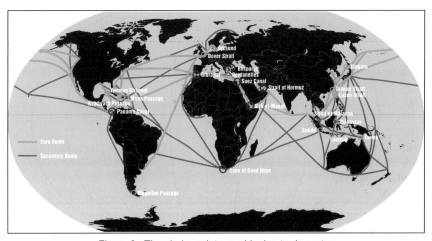

Figure 3. The choke points on shipping trade routes

Shipping 'choke points'

When we examine the flow of trade by ship there are some points where the traffic is squeezed into relatively narrow channels in order to take the shortest route available or to reach ports in sea areas which are almost surrounded by land. These have become channels of both opportunity and of risk. The opportunity is for providers of services for ships; the risk is the navigational risk of many ships travelling in a restricted space and also the risk that nation states or criminals might choose to exert leverage by intercepting ships or by restricting free passage. The best known of these 'choke points' are, in no special order:

The English Channel

The Skaw

The Strait of Gibraltar

The Dardanelles and Bosphorus

The Suez Canal

The Strait of Hormuz

The Strait of Malacca

The Panama Canal.

Two other choke points are the Cape of Good Hope at the tip of South Africa and Cape Horn at the tip of South America, where vessels sail close to the shore to avoid wild weather to the south.

Cargo flow

Ship operators want to keep their vessels carrying cargo (laden voyage) for as long as possible; they do not earn any money when the vessel has no cargo (ballast voyage). Their ability to do this depends on whether there is a suitable cargo available at a port near to where they discharge their cargo (discharge port). For big bulk carriers and big tankers this is difficult to achieve. The smaller vessels have a better chance as whilst the cargo they have to discharge is required at or near the discharge port, there will probably be another cargo, for which the vessel is suitable, at a nearby port. When you look at diagrams of cargo flow, they generally show the flow of the largest cargo and will not reflect the long voyages in ballast that the operator has to undertake to return to a loading area.

One interesting feature of this topic for container ships is that there is more cargo flowing from East to West so, in theory, we could eventually run out of containers. As a consequence, many of the containers onboard vessels going East are 'empties' being returned for a new cargo.

Some cargo flows are very dependent on seasons. There are clear seasons for shipping fruit out of Central America, so the refrigerated vessels in this trade need to find alternative employment out of season.

The issue of seasonality also affects some product tanker trades and bulk carriers, especially those involved in the grain trade.

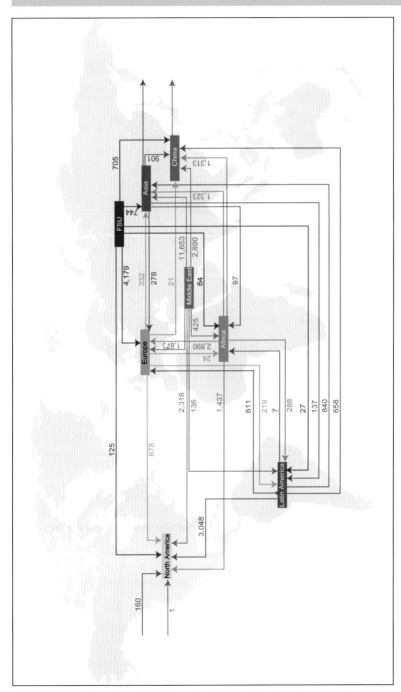

Figure 4. World crude oil exports by destination 2012 (1,000 b/d)

Image courtesy of OPEC (www.opec.org)

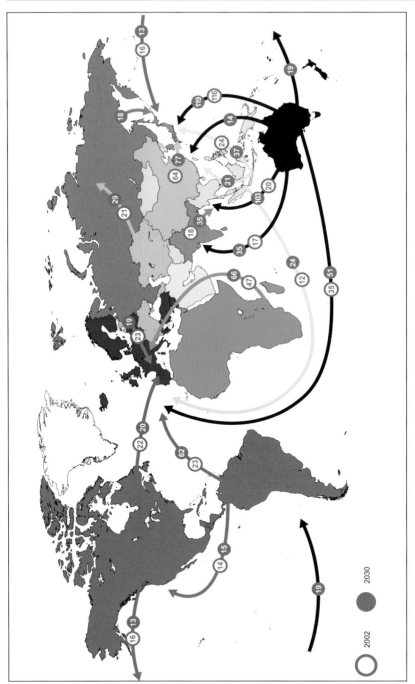

Figure 5. Coal trade flow by origin and destination - million tonnes per year

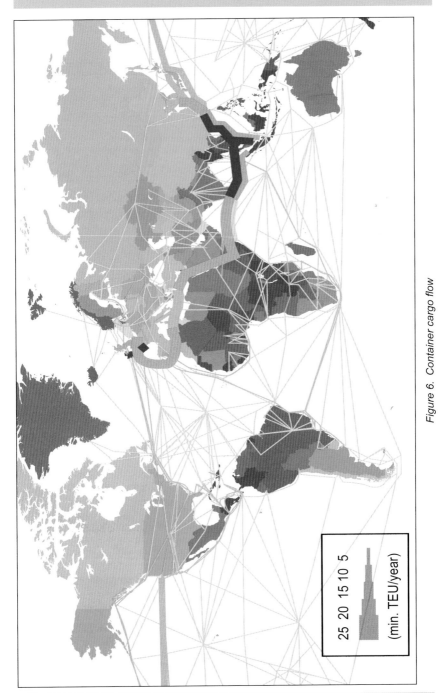

Figure 6. Container cargo flow

25 20 15 10 5

(min. TEU/year)

Chapter 2 - Ship fundamentals

How ships float

A ship hull has a volume, depending on its shape, and a mass (weight), depending on the material of construction and the contents inside the vessel (including machinery, cargo, people, etc.).

If a ship is lowered into water, the volume of the ship below the surface of the water displaces – or pushes out of the way – the water to make space for the hull. The amount displaced will be the same as the mass of the ship. If the ship displaces its mass before the water level overflows into the hull then the ship floats. If the ship is so heavy that the water reaches the top of the hull and overflows into the ship, the ship sinks.

Because a lot of the hull volume is air, even though the ship is made of steel it will usually float well before the water reaches the top. The distance between the water when the ship is floating and the top of the hull is called the 'freeboard', and this is the sailor's safety margin. To ensure that unscrupulous operators do not 'overload' a ship, every ship has marks painted on the hull showing the maximum depth to which the ship can be loaded; this is called the load line or Plimsoll mark (after the British Member of Parliament Samuel Plimsoll who established the law in 1876 which regulates this).

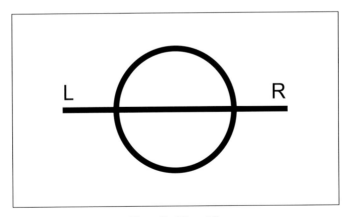

Figure 7. Plimsoll line

To allow for water of different density (salt, brackish, fresh) and to allow for different weather conditions, additional marks have been used to give a more consistent load line for different situations. This is regulated by the International Convention on Load Lines (as amended from 1930 to date).

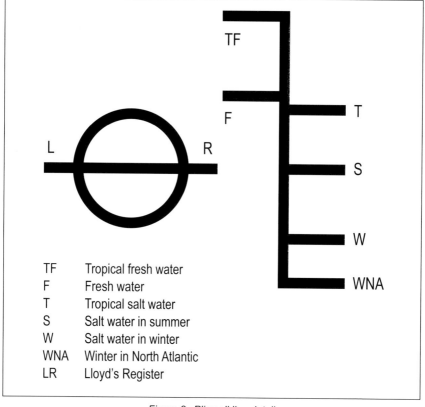

TF   Tropical fresh water
F   Fresh water
T   Tropical salt water
S   Salt water in summer
W   Salt water in winter
WNA Winter in North Atlantic
LR   Lloyd's Register

Figure 8. Plimsoll line detail

When you see a remark stating that a ship has a summer deadweight (DWT) of 50,000 tonnes, this means the ship can carry a total weight of cargo, bunker fuel, stores and water of 50,000 tonnes and, in salt water, the load line will just be touching the surface of the water.

Why ships stay upright

Every solid object has a centre of gravity (or, more correctly, a centre of mass). It is a point at which, if supported from directly beneath that point, it will balance.

In the example in Fig. 9 you can see the centre of gravity of my ship. Every floating object has a centre of buoyancy; this is the centre of the volume of water displaced by the hull. The centre of gravity is right above the centre of buoyancy when the ship is upright.

If the ship heels over (heeling over means the vessel rolls over towards one side, and this is caused by wind or wave action) because the shape of the displaced water volume has changed, the centre of buoyancy moves and this shift pushes the ship upright once again.

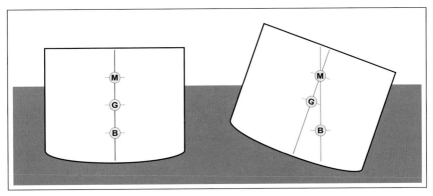

Figure 9. Stability diagram

In the diagram you can see a point marked 'M'; this is called the metacentre, and for small angles of heel this position is fixed. The distance between the centre of gravity and the metacentre is called the metacentric height and this determines if the ship will be 'stiff', in which case it recovers from a heel very quickly, or 'tender', which involves a much gentler recovery.

In general, tankers and bulk carriers are stiff ships, which means they can be 'uncomfortable' but they are generally very stable. Passenger ships and warships can be very tender and comfortable but there is a need for care to ensure they remain stable.

If ships have tanks with a large surface area containing liquids (e.g. cargo tanks on tankers, ballast tanks on all ships), there is a risk that the movement of the liquid in these tanks could affect the stability of the ship. This is called the 'free surface' effect. You can get some idea of this effect by placing four full pint glasses on a deep tray and carrying the tray across a room. Then, pour the contents of all four glasses into the tray, remove the glasses and walk back. The walk back will be very difficult with the liquid seeming to have a life of its own. This is why tanks are sub-divided to minimise the free surface.

Why do ships sink?

If a ship reaches a point where the buoyancy is not enough to counteract the weight of the whole ship and cargo, it will sink. At this point, the water will be above the main deck and will enter the inside of the hull through any available opening. Because ships are only loaded to the load line, there is a considerable height of hull above the water (the freeboard) so a ship will usually only sink because of a loss of buoyancy or loss of stability. The major cause of loss of buoyancy is a collision with another ship or structure that makes a hole in the hull, or a grounding, where the ship hits the seabed and this punches a hole in the hull.

Ships' hulls are divided into watertight compartments arranged so that if one or more compartments are broken open to the sea, those compartments not breached will continue to provide buoyancy and keep the ship afloat (as long as not too many compartments are damaged). The loss of stability can cause the ship to list (heel over to one side due to the shift in the centre of gravity caused by a shift of weight) so far that the main deck dips under the water. This has the effect of increasing the weight of the whole ship (because of the weight of the water that has flowed into spaces where it should not be). If a ship lists too far, the cargo can shift to the side, making the list worse; this is a significant problem with dry bulk cargo, especially on smaller coastal ships which only have a small number of cargo holds.

Ship dimensions

Describing a ship

> The front of a ship is called the bow or the stem.
>
> The back of a ship is called the stern.
>
> The left hand side of the ship (looking towards the bow) is the Port side.
>
> The right hand side of the ship (looking towards the bow) is the Starboard side.
>
> The main body of the ship is called the hull.
>
> The principal highest watertight deck is called the main deck.
>
> The 'buildings' above the main deck are called the superstructure.
>
> The lowest part of the hull is called the keel.

Will the car fit in the garage?

Because of the need to ensure that ships can navigate shallow waters, fit alongside berths, sail underneath bridges and fit the required cargo onboard, there are a large number of measurements which are needed for the operation and chartering of ships. It is important to realise that one of these measurements, the draught, can change when the ship moves from one type of water to another – from salt to fresh water when entering a river or from salt to brackish when entering some harbours. A change in air draught because of a change in draught will affect the clearance when sailing under a bridge, as will the changes in water level through the action of the tides.

Diagram of vessel dimensions

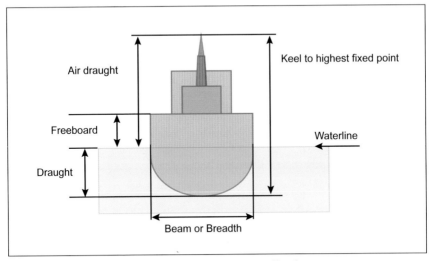

Figure 10. Shipping diagram (front)

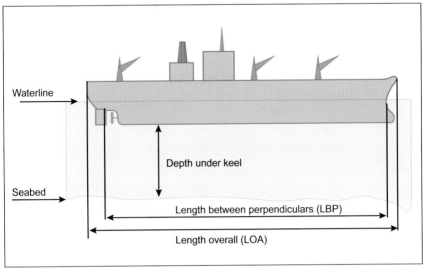

Figure 11. Shipping diagram (side)

Table of vessel dimensions

Vessel dimensions		
Air draught	Highest point to actual waterline	
AP	After perpendicular	Line perpendicular to the rudder post
10 bar	-125°C	Storage on ship in Type C tanks
BCM	Bow to centre of manifold	Tankers only
Beam	Breadth at the widest point	
Displacement (actual)	Total weight of ship	At a particular loaded condition
Displacement (maximum)	Total weight of ship	Loaded to summer deadweight
Draught	Bottom of hull to actual waterline	
DWT	Deadweight tonnage	Maximum weight of cargo, bunkers, stores and water a vessel can carry
FP	Forward perpendicular	Line perpendicular to where the loaded waterline cuts the bow
Freeboard	Main deck to the actual waterline	
GRT	Gross registered tonnage (obsolete)	Formula calculation of enclosed volume of vessel
GT	Gross tonnage	Formula calculation of enclosed volume of vessel
KHFP	Keel to highest fixed point	
KTM	Keel to masthead	
LBP	Length between perpendiculars	Length between the forward and after perpendiculars
LOA	Length overall	
M	Ship's rail to manifold	
MH	Manifold height above main deck	
NRT	Net registered tonnage (obsolete)	Formula calculation of volume of cargo-carrying space

NT	Net tonnage	Formula calculation of volume of cargo-carrying space
PBL	Parallel body length	Length of flat side at loaded waterline
SCM	Stern to centre of manifold	Tankers only

For tankers, this information is usually provided as part of a questionnaire, called Q88, which contains additional information needed with regard to cargo tanks, cargo heating, etc.

For other vessels, the operator will provide any dimensions required by the charterer or other counterparty.

For some operations such as berthing at a quay, mooring to a single point mooring or preparing to receive bunkers (especially for unusual ships, heavy lift vessels with cargo onboard or drilling rigs), much detailed planning will be required.

Tonnage

The measurement of ship size is worthy of a book on its own but the fundamental requirement is how much can the ship carry and how will the port assess any charges due. The first method was to identify the volume of cargo the ship could carry and this was the number of standard barrels of goods that could be fitted into the hold. The barrels were called tuns, and so we ended up with a volume in tuns of 252 gallons. By the 18th century, this had been replaced by a simple calculation based on length and breadth. This gave the 'gross tonnage' (GT) of the ship. Once steamships started to displace sailing ships, an allowance had to be made when assessing port charges for the amount of space used for purposes other than cargo space. This gave us 'net tonnage' (the cargo-carrying volume).

For warships and passenger vessels, the usual measurement is 'displacement tonnage', which is the actual weight of the ship and cargo. This is the empty ship (lightship weight) plus the cargo, bunkers, stores and water (the DWT).

Beware that today the gross tonnage and net tonnage have no units and are complex calculations, the DWT and lightship weight are in tonnes and the displacement is in tonnes. Both the Suez Canal and the Panama Canal have their own unique tonnage measurement systems for calculating the transit fees.

Chapter 3 - Ship types

Cargo ship arrangement

The traditional cargo ship was designed with its engine room in the middle of the hull with the living accommodation on top above the main deck and the space for cargo (cargo holds) arranged in front and behind the engine room. A standard arrangement was three holds in front of the engine room and two behind. The shaft for driving the propeller had to run, in a separate compartment (the shaft tunnel), from the engine room to the stern, underneath the after holds.

This arrangement permitted the vessel to float on an 'even keel' even when empty of cargo.

These ships had simple cranes (called derricks) to allow them to discharge and load in those ports which did not have cranes. The cargo holds were closed and made watertight by cargo hatches (originally these were wooden planks covered with tarpaulin sheets). There was often an additional space immediately below the main hatches called the 'tween deck' which provided additional stowage space. Over the last 40 years, the use of 'tween deck' spaces has diminished and metal hatch covers have been introduced which are mechanically folded to give access for working cargo.

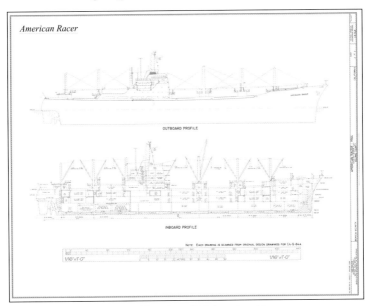

Figure 12. Elevation of SS American Racer

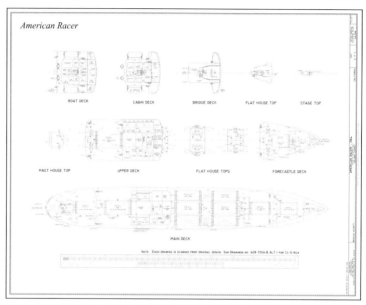

Figure 13. Plan of SS American Racer

The *American Racer* was typical of the high-speed break bulk cargo ships of her era. She was delivered in November 1964 to United States Lines. She could carry refrigerated cargo as well as break bulk cargo and she had a limited number of 'cell guides' to allow her to carry some containers. She was a notable ship for her time, heavily automated, with bridge control of her main steam turbine engines and a 'reduced' crew of 39 (compared to 60 on her non-automated sisters).

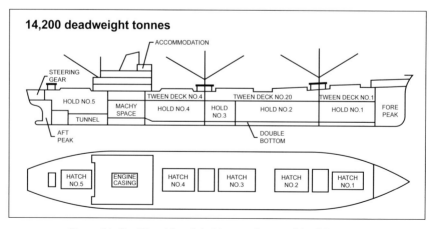

Figure 14. Traditional 'break bulk' general cargo ship of the 1970s

Tankers and then bulk carriers were designed with the engine room at the after end of the ship so that the propeller shaft did not run beneath the cargo holds. This made the fitting of cargo pipelines and the emptying of the tanks much easier. Until the early 1960s, these vessels still had some crew accommodation in the middle of the ship. This was to place the wheelhouse in a position which gave the deck officers a good view over the bow.

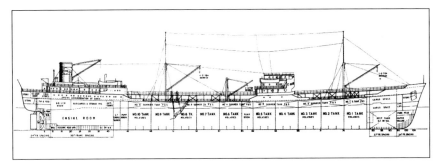

Figure 15. Traditional 1950s oil tanker

In the 1960s, all the living accommodation was placed at the after end, above the engine room, and the height of the accommodation was arranged to give a good view from the wheelhouse. This arrangement meant that if the vessel was empty of cargo, the stern was always much deeper in the water than the bow, although this could be corrected by taking on water ballast – either in the cargo tanks or in special ballast tanks.

A tanker will have its cargo space divided into many separate tanks (from 10 up to 36), either two or three abreast, and connected to the cargo pipelines to permit cargo operation. The tanks all have cargo tank hatches on the main deck to allow visual inspection and access for maintenance. These tank hatches are usually kept closed by oil-tight tank lids, and they are much smaller than the cargo hatches on general cargo or bulk cargo ships.

The use of multiple tanks provides three key advantages. First, the sub-divided tanks create a very strong hull, making tankers amongst the safest ships at sea. Second, the incorporation of many small tanks has a much less negative effect on the stability of the ship at sea than one or two tanks (see remarks on *Free surface effect*). Third, the use of many tanks permits the simultaneous carriage of a number of different grades of cargo at the same time. All tankers now have a 'double hull' to reduce the risk of oil pollution.

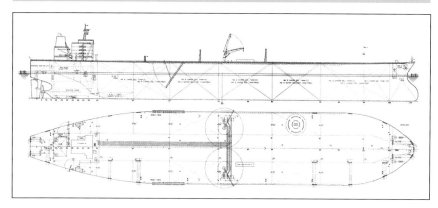

Figure 16. Double hull modern VLCC

Bulk carriers have their holds arranged in line from forward to aft, stretching the full width of the ship. They will have a double bottom between the bottom of the cargo holds and the bottom of the ship. Larger bulk carriers have sloping sides to their holds (at the top and the bottom) to assist with cargo handling, and the hatch covers on the biggest bulk carriers are so big they can be used as a helicopter landing pad when closed. The hatch covers on smaller vessels fold in sections from forward to aft (folding hatch covers) whilst on the big vessels they slide to the side of the ship (side-rolling hatch covers).

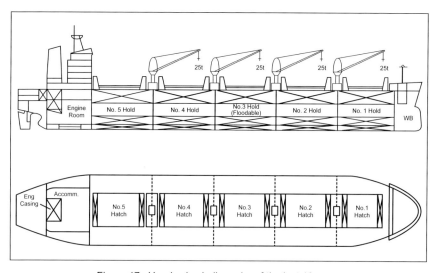

Figure 17. Handy size bulk carrier of the last 10 years

It is common for bulldozers and loader vehicles to be lowered into the holds of large bulk carriers near the end of the discharge to allow shore grabs to reach all of the remaining cargo; this is one reason for the very large hatch openings. Smaller bulk carriers often have cranes to allow them to load and discharge their own cargo.

By the mid-1970s, most cargo ships were arranged with the engine room and the living accommodation at the stern.

On some ships, the accommodation and the wheelhouse are situated well forward, close to the bow. This can be seen in specialist cargo vessels and offshore support vessels either because of a need to have a large open deck area for deck cargo or because of a requirement for a very high degree of forward visibility for manoeuvring. However, these vessels will still have their engine room near the stern, especially if they have a direct shaft from the engines to the propellers. Offshore support vessels will have their engines under the accommodation as there is insufficient room under the cargo deck.

General cargo

General cargo ships have been the work horses of the oceans for centuries, carrying every kind of cargo. Currently, there are about 14,000 general cargo ships over 1,000 DWT. However, since specialist ships such as tankers, bulk carriers and refrigerated cargo ships arrived at the beginning of the 20th century, the general cargo ship has lost its place and now represents a much smaller percentage of total tonnage.

General cargo vessels usually have the equipment onboard to load and discharge their own cargo and their holds can be configured to carry a very large range of cargo. Their non-specialised nature makes them suitable for changing cargo type, trading route and sailing speed from one voyage to the next, and they are often referred to as 'tramp' ships, with their owners looking for voyages which will minimise the amount of time the vessels spend in ballast condition.

The smallest general cargo ships are coasters, designed for short voyages along the coast or for short sea operation, calling internationally but on voyages lasting just a few days.

General cargo ships are sometimes called 'break bulk' ships. Their cargo may be goods in bales (especially textiles or raw materials like cotton), boxes, barrels, drums, bags or sacks (especially grain) or single items of equipment (cars, machinery, etc.). The term comes from 'breaking bulk', where some of the cargo is removed and discharged ashore whilst the remainder remains onboard for another quay or another port. This is the traditional method of cargo carriage, only superseded with the advent of the oil tanker, the bulk carrier and, finally, the container ship.

Up until the 1970s, there were many large general cargo ships which operated a 'liner trade', much like the large container ships of today. A liner trade is one where the vessel follows a fixed route with programmed calls at the ports en route according to a timetable; it is used by container shipping, reefer shipping and some car carriers. It is a labour intensive method of loading and discharging but is still very useful for ports that lack the infrastructure to handle more specialised vessels.

Figure 18. General cargo ship

Photograph courtesy of Nigel Draffin

Specialist dry cargo

This type of ship, whilst often engaged in tramping, is one whose design and construction is specifically suited to a particular kind of cargo. Some of these vessels are involved with the transport of 'project cargo' – large pieces of equipment for construction projects or plant installations. Such cargoes need the vessel to have considerable versatility in the use of available cargo space to permit loading, stowage and discharge of unusual shapes, extreme weights and extreme sizes of cargo.

Car carriers

These vessels have extensive vehicle decks and loading ramps (at the stern and at the side) that permit vehicles to be driven onto the vessels to be stowed and lashed in 'lanes' along the vehicle decks. The decks often have the ability to be raised to allow the stowage of double height vehicles. The vehicles are then driven off once the vessel has reached the discharge port. The whole cargo is stored inside the hull and superstructure of the vessel.

Car carriers have a very high freeboard and strong winds can make them difficult to handle. The ship size is usually measured in available deck area in square metres (m^2)(ranging from 12,000 m^2 to 65,000 m^2) or by the number of cars (ranging from 1,200 to 8,000 cars). Whilst the side ramp usually has a weight limit of 10-20 tonnes, the stern ramp is often much stronger, capable of taking weights of 120-150 tonnes. This allows the vessels to carry project cargo as long as the height is less than about 5 metres (m) and the cargo can be rolled onboard. Car carriers are usually measured by their capacity in car equivalent units (CEU) or 'lane metres'.

Roll-on Roll-off (Ro-Ro)

These ships are an adaption of the car carrier. Their cargo is also driven on and off the ship using ramps but the cargo, whilst on wheels, can be towed on and off the vessel by tractor units that are kept ashore at ports. Some Ro-Ro ships have an open deck area towards the stern; cargo stowed here must be protected against the weather. They are often used to carry project cargo as long as it will fit onto wheeled low-level trailers. They are also extensively used for the ferry service of large road trucks, especially tractor/trailer units. In this instance, the 'tractor' will stay behind at the load port and a different tractor at the discharge port will retrieve the trailer.

Figure 19. Ro-Ro vessel

Photograph courtesy of Nigel Draffin

Heavy lift

These vessels are equipped with high capacity cranes to allow the lifting of very heavy cargo. On a heavy lift ship, the crane capacity will be up to many hundreds of tonnes and the vessel will also be equipped with a sophisticated arrangement of ballast tanks and pumps to control the stability of the vessel during the lifting and lowering of the cargo. The vessel personnel have to take great care in lifting, lowering and stowing the cargo because of stability issues, and this means that the cargo operations have to be planned in great detail and well in advance.

Figure 20. Heavy lift ship

Photograph courtesy of Nigel Draffin

Dock ships

These vessels are an adaption of the heavy lift concept. A dock ship is constructed with a well deck that takes up nearly 75% of the vessel's deck area. This well deck can accept huge cargoes, complete ships, drilling rigs and other objects that could not normally be transported. If the cargo is one that can float (such as another vessel or a floating drilling rig), then the dock ship can ballast down so that the well deck is completely submerged with only the superstructure remaining above the water and the cargo can be floated onto the dock ship. The ballast will then be pumped out causing the dock ship to rise up beneath the cargo, letting it sit on the well deck and lifting the cargo above the level of the water. These vessels can carry cargo that is wider than the dock ship.

Figure 21. Dock ship Blue Marlin *with* Ocean Monarch

Photograph courtesy of Dockwise (www.dockwise.com)

Tankers

Tankers carry liquid cargo in bulk, almost anything from cryogenic liquid gas at -162°C to bitumen at 150°C. They are used for oil, gas, orange juice, chemicals, molten sulphur – in fact, almost any liquid. A tanker's cargo space is divided into a number of separate cargo tanks with a pipeline system that permits the tanks to be loaded and discharged individually. Some cargo requires specially-shaped tanks, insulated tanks and tanks which can cope with high internal pressure. The complexity of the pipelines and pumping systems depends on the type of cargo the ship will carry. Many tankers require special provisions for safety and for cargo care – a controlled atmosphere above the cargo (inert gas), heating coils, refrigeration, etc. – and they are subject to very strict regulation. The first tankers in 1890 were only 4,000 DWT; the largest ever built were 550,000 DWT and were built in the 1970s.

Oil

Figure 22. The Batillus *tanker in Saint-Nazaire*

Photograph attributed to Jacques Girard

The biggest tanker ever (at the time of building) was the *SS Batillus* at 553,662 DWT. Built in 1976, she was an ultra large crude carrier (ULCC).

In Fig. 22 she is taking on bunkers from a 14,000 DWT tanker after completing initial sea trials. The photograph was taken in 1976 but the vessel was scrapped in 1985; she and her three sisters were never economically viable.

There are about 4,500 oil tankers over 1,000 DWT. Oil tankers are usually divided into 'clean' and 'dirty', depending on the nature of the cargo they are intended to carry, and also into 'product tankers' or 'crude tankers'. Clean products might be gasoline, naphtha or jet fuel; dirty products are fuel oil and crude oil.

Product tankers, both clean and dirty, range from a few hundred DWT up to about 100,000 DWT, whilst crude tankers range from about 70,000 DWT to about 420,000 DWT. Most will have shared cargo pipelines with cargo pumps in a separate pump room and will have a limited number of different oil grades that can be carried simultaneously without contamination (so-called grade segregation). Some smaller vessels will have one or more pumps in each tank and a greater number of segregation possibilities. The following table gives the principal size groups and indicates if they have the ability to heat their cargo.

Tanker size table

Vessel description	Maximum size DWT	Clean (C), dirty (D) or both (B)	Heating	Comments
GP	25,000	C	No	Clean product tanker
GP	25,000	B	Yes	General purpose
MR	50,000	B	Yes	Medium range
LR1	85,000	B	Yes	Aframax
LR2	150,000	D	Yes	Suezmax
VLCC	320,000	D	No	Very Large Crude Carrier
ULCC	450,000	D	No	Ultra Large Crude Carrier

Figure 23. Coastal tanker

Photograph courtesy of Nigel Draffin

Gas

These are tankers that carry gas as a liquid in their tanks. The cargo has to be kept at a temperature and pressure that allows the cargo to remain as a liquid. The principal division is between liquefied natural gas (LNG) and liquefied petroleum gas (LPG). Both groups usually require the cargo to be kept cold but they use different techniques for this and some smaller LPG vessels can carry their cargo at atmospheric temperature but under considerable pressure.

The extreme low temperatures require special materials to be used and the vessels are built to very high standards with rigorous safety standards. Gas carrier size is usually measured by the volume of cargo the ship can carry expressed in cubic metres (m^3).

LNG

There are currently around 360 LNG tankers in service. This cargo is predominantly composed of methane and is carried just above atmospheric pressure and at a temperature of -162°C. Whilst the ship is carrying the cargo, heat will leak in through the insulated cargo tank and cause the LNG to 'boil off', which could raise the pressure in the tank to unsafe levels. The removal of the boil off gas helps to keep the cargo cool, as the action of boiling requires continuous inflow of heat.

The boil off is normally removed and piped to the engine room where it is used as fuel for the ship, although some vessels have equipment that allows them to refrigerate the boil off, turning it back to liquid (re-liquefaction). The vessels either have large spherical tanks that protrude from the main deck or special designs of prismatic tanks that are below the main deck. The smallest are 20,000 m^3 capacity and the largest 265,000 m^3 capacity.

Figure 24. The Arctic Princess *LNG tanker*

LPG

There are some 870 LPG ships currently in service. These LPG tankers face the same problems as LNG vessels but the temperatures at atmospheric pressure for the gases are much higher. Butane boils at -1°C, propane at - 42°C and ethylene at -104°C. If they are carried at a higher pressure, then the temperatures will be higher. The boil off gas cannot be used in the engine room so it is either contained (at a high pressure) on small ships or re-liquefied and returned to the tank as liquid. Currently, there are around 300 ships of up to 10,000 m³ capacity categorised as pressurised (no refrigeration) and about 355 ships of up to 16,000 m³ capacity categorised as semi-refrigerated (raised pressure and some re-liquefaction). There are also about 215 ships of up to 85,000 m³ capacity which are fully-refrigerated (all boil off re-liquefied).

Figure 25. LPG pressurised tanker

Photograph courtesy of Nigel Draffin

Chemical

Chemical tankers are specialised tankers designed for the carriage of any bulk liquid chemicals detailed in Chapter 17 of the International Code for the Construction and Equipment of Ships carrying Dangerous Chemicals in Bulk (IBC Code). The chemicals will be stored in tanks with special protective coatings or made from stainless steel, and the tankers will have tank-heating systems, cargo pumps situated in each tank, and dedicated pipeline systems for each tank.

Bulk carriers

There are about 5,000 bulk carriers of over 1,000 DWT. These vessels are designed to carry one type of bulk commodity at a time. They may have some cargo handling equipment but most are designed to be loaded and discharged using shore-based equipment. The different ship sizes are described in the table below. Ships are described as 'geared' if they have their own cranes to handle the cargo loading and discharge, or 'gearless' if they do not have their own cranes.

Bulk carrier size table

Vessel description	Typical size DWT	Geared	Comments
Handy size	30,000	Yes	General purpose bulker
Handymax	55,000	Yes	General purpose bulker
Panamax	70,000	Yes	Largest size for Panama Canal
Capesize	175,000	No	Large bulk carrier
VLOC	300,000	No	Very Large Ore Carrier
Valemax	400,000	No	Largest bulker design to date

Figure 26. Handy size bulker

Photograph courtesy of Nigel Draffin

Coal/iron ore/bauxite

This type of bulker is the predominant type in the Capesize and larger sectors. They are very rarely fitted with their own cargo handling equipment and the cargo holds are covered with very large side-rolling hatches to provide easy access for the discharging grabs or buckets (each one lifting up to 85 tonnes (60 m³)). The ships have ballast tanks in double bottom spaces beneath the holds and in 'hopper' ballast tanks either side of the holds. Vessels designed for iron ore are specially strengthened whilst those for lighter cargo, such as coal, can carry iron ore in alternate holds, each of these having strengthened bottoms.

Grain

This is a routine cargo for smaller bulkers up to Panamax size. It is carried in both geared and gearless ships. The discharge may be undertaken with grabs or with screw elevators lowered into the holds in the discharge port.

Timber products

This kind of bulker bridges the gap between the conventional bulk carrier and the general cargo ship. These vessels are used to transport a huge range of timber and forest products, and they can carry, and are often fitted with, gantry cranes which can traverse the entire length of the cargo deck. They have folding hatch covers and can carry containers on top of the hatches. They can also carry a large range of 'unitised' cargo in their holds.

Container ships

Container ships appeared as a new addition to world shipping in the 1950s. Although the concept had been developed by railway companies in the 1930s, it did not gain attention until the efforts of Malcolm McLean, who developed the metal shipping container (or 'box') that could be transported by truck and train, and stacked one on top of another onboard ship.

It took years to build the port infrastructure but by 1970 the shipping world had changed as the great cargo liners gave way to new ships carrying up to 2,000 of the 20-foot long boxes (also known as twenty-foot equivalent units (TEU)). The containers sit inside holds, supported by rails called cell guides, with more boxes stacked on top of the hatch covers until reaching up to five boxes high above the main deck.

Some vessels are built without normal hatch covers but they have to meet special rules on hull strength and on pumping water out of the holds. The small ships have their own cranes for loading and discharging but larger vessels rely on shore cranes to move the boxes. Many of the containers used today are forty-foot equivalent units (FEU), this being the optimum size internationally for road transport and rail transport. At present, the biggest ships have a capacity of 18,000 TEU. As each new size record is broken, the preceding class is downgraded to operate on shorter trade routes, with small ships of 1,500-2,000 TEU acting as feeder ships from the smallest ports.

There are containers equipped with refrigeration units for the carriage of perishable goods and others containing cylindrical tanks for carrying liquids, all with the same dimensional footprint. The 18,000 TEU M-class A.P.Møller-Maersk vessels are currently the largest cargo ships in the world. Propulsion is provided by two 30 megawatt (MW) diesel engines yet each vessel only has a crew of 12.

There are about 160 container ships over 10,000 TEU capacity out of a total fleet of 6,000 container vessels. The top 20 players in this market control about 3,400 vessels with an average capacity of about 4,400 TEU. There are over 2,500 smaller container ships with an average capacity of about 700 TEU.

Container ships have particular hazards if the contents of each container are described incorrectly. The shipper must identify the contents, describe any hazardous cargo and, most importantly, give an accurate description of the weight of the loaded container. Many instances of the loss of containers over the side of the ship have been as a consequence of weight being wrongly described, leading to heavy containers being stowed above deck on top of lighter containers.

Container vessel size table

Vessel description	Typical size TEU	Geared	Comments
Small feeder	1,000	Yes	Small feeder ship
Feeder	2,000	Yes	Feeder ship
Feedermax	3,000	Yes	Largest feeder size
Panamax	5,100	No	Largest size for Panama Canal
Post Panamax	10,000	No	Too big for Panama Canal (pre-expansion)
New Panamax	14,500	No	Maximum size for new Panama expansion
ULCV	18,000	No	Ultra large container vessel

Figure 27. Container small geared feeder

Photograph courtesy of Nigel Draffin

Figure 28. Container ship

Photograph courtesy of Nigel Draffin

Refrigerated ships

At present, there are about 900 dedicated refrigerator (reefer) ships in service. Whilst container ships now carry a proportion of the refrigerated cargo, the bulk still goes by dedicated reefers. These vessels not only keep each hold section at the optimum temperature for each cargo, they also monitor and control the atmosphere (oxygen, carbon monoxide, carbon dioxide and nitrogen) to ensure that the fruit and vegetable cargo arrives at exactly the degree of ripeness required by the buyer. The economy of scale allows frozen meat cargo to arrive in perfect condition irrespective of journey time (although reefer ships are amongst the fastest in service). These vessels have very large refrigeration plant and complex hold ventilation systems. Some reefer cargo trades are very seasonal so the vessels will also carry other cargo and can carry containers.

Figure 29. Atlantic Klipper *reefer vessel*

Photograph courtesy of Seatrade (www.seatrade.com)

Figure 30. The Salica Frigo

Photograph courtesy of Clipper (CC BY 2.5)

Traditionally, reefer ships were painted white and were very fast (operating at over 20 knots). Many modern reefers look like conventional container ships. However, the holds below the main deck are fitted out for carrying cargo on pallets and the holds are insulated and refrigerated. The containers stored above deck can be refrigerated or conventional containers.

Passenger ships

Passenger shipping was the most significant means of international travel until the arrival of mass air travel in the late 1950s. After a complete downturn in the sector, the shipping industry transitioned from just offering passenger transport to also providing passenger entertainment and, with the advent of the cruise liner, there are probably more people at sea than there have ever been.

Passenger shipping is more closely regulated than any other sector and the first international shipping convention was produced in the wake of the loss of the *Titanic* in 1912. This convention then evolved to become the International Convention for the Safety of Life at Sea (SOLAS). Modern passenger ships now dwarf the ocean liners of the mid-20th century, but their role has changed from transport to leisure and they spend half of their time moored, or anchored outside ports, waiting for their passengers to return from excursions. Many of the lifeboats fitted to cruise liners are constructed so as to allow them to be used as tenders to ferry passengers to and from shore excursions.

Liners

There are only two large passenger liners left in service (*Queen Mary II* and *Marco Polo* (now sailing as a cruise liner)), with one more on order (*Titanic II*). They spend much of their year in alternative roles as cruise vessels; the difference between the two vessel types is that a liner needs speed and comfort on an extended passage at sea.

Figure 31. The QE2 *at South Queensferry*

Photograph courtesy of Tim Dyer

The *Queen Elizabeth 2* (*QE2*) liner, now retired, was designed as luxury transport rather than a floating holiday venue.

Cruise vessels

Currently, there are about 800 ocean-going cruise ships in operation. Cruise ships today are vast floating resorts; the smallest will carry 500 passengers and 400 crew, and the largest, 4,000 passengers plus 2,000 crew. They generally operate in very specific areas – the Caribbean, the Mediterranean, the Baltic, and the South China Sea. Cruise ships often spend their steaming time moving at slow speed from port to port overnight, only using their full speed on the first and last day of each cruise. Their design focus is on 'cargo care', keeping their passengers fed, entertained and happy.

Figure 32. The MS Majesty of the Seas

Photograph courtesy of Matt H. Wade (CC BY 3.0)

Ferries

Ferries are the simplest and most economical link between ports on short sea routes for both passengers and vehicular traffic. The smallest ferries in international trade are those running between the islands in the Baltic Sea. Some ferries carry only a few cars and trucks plus passengers, while others carry many hundreds of cars and over 1,000 passengers. Some of the ferries operating in the Mediterranean are very high speed and high tech.

Figure 33. High speed ferry underway

Photograph courtesy of Nigel Draffin

Figure 34. Passenger ferry

Photograph courtesy of Nigel Draffin

Offshore vessels

Offshore vessels provide services to companies engaged in projects 'at sea'. They ferry personnel and equipment to these locations, providing a floating platform for technicians and scientists, and rendering assistance to other vessels. The first four types detailed here will share many features and are, in general, almost interchangeable, but they will have some features specific to their particular roles and specialisation.

Oil field support

These vessels ferry personnel, fuel, supplies, equipment and stores to enable the continuous operation of exploration and oil production facilities. They range between 1,000-5,000 DWT and are designed to work in extreme weather conditions. Most of them have a very large open deck aft of the superstructure for carriage of deck cargo. This deck is also used to assist in anchoring floating rigs (anchor handling). These are called anchor handling tug supply (AHTS) vessels. They have propellers and thrusters that can direct their thrust to push the ship sideways as well as ahead and astern. Their operation is linked to sophisticated controls that allow the ship to maintain its position at a fixed spot by balancing the thrust from the different propellers and thrusters, even in extreme weather (dynamic positioning).

A vessel's capability in dynamic positioning is indicated as DP1, DP2 or DP3. The higher the number, the more sophisticated the capability, and DP3 vessels can hold position under automatic control with a high degree of redundancy. This latter class is required when working in close proximity to offshore structures, working with divers receiving support from the vessel (either directly attached to the vessel with an umbilical cord providing breathing support, power and data links, or working from a diving bell on the sea floor).

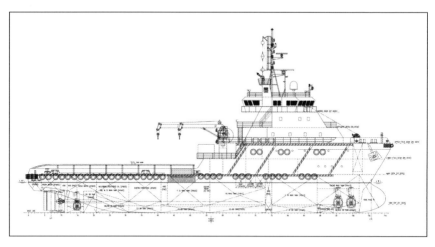

Figure 35. Modern anchor handling tug supply vessel (AHTS)

Photograph courtesy of MAN Diesel & Turbo (www.mandieselturbo.com)

Diving support vessels

Divers working underwater for extended periods and at depths greater than 30 m require a measure of technical and equipment support. When working below 100 m, the risks of medical complications when returning to the surface have led to the development of 'saturation diving', where the divers not only breathe special gas mixtures but also spend very long periods in a pressurised environment between their diving tasks. When this work is underway the divers will be supported by a specialist diving support vessel.

The vessels are equipped with all the equipment needed to allow divers to work under the sea at depths where they need life support systems to keep them safe, such as breathing support, power and data links. They will have the ability to launch, service and recover a diving bell, and support its systems whilst it is on the sea floor. They also provide an onboard decompression chamber to allow divers to recover from working at great depths, as well as 'hyperbaric' lifeboats, permitting the divers in decompression to transfer to a lifeboat whilst still under controlled pressure conditions in the case of an onboard emergency.

Most diving support vessels will have a 'helideck' to permit a helicopter to land and take off for personnel and equipment transfers. Many of these vessels will also have cranes suitable for handling large equipment.

Offshore survey and engineering

These vessels are used for different types of undersea surveying, the most common being side-scan sonar and acoustic seismic survey. They map the ocean floor and the geological structure beneath it. To do this they must travel at slow speed along an exact route, often towing a long trail of 'hydrophones' to pick up the returns from the seabed. They need a lot of power for their size and will often have a dynamic positioning capability. Some of them (offshore engineering vessels) are used to dig or plough trenches in the seabed for laying pipelines or cables.

This class also includes specialist pipe-laying vessels and undersea mining vessels. They are also used to handle large pieces of sub-sea equipment, lowering them from, and raising them to, the surface as part of project support duties. This requires not only dynamic positioning capabilities but also sophisticated ballast and tensioning winch systems to compensate for vessel movement whilst working.

These ships are used to deploy and operate unmanned remotely operated underwater vehicles (ROV) which can perform mechanical maintenance tasks and record images deep underwater. Sometimes the vessels have an opening in the bottom of the hull from which an unmanned ROV or manned mini-submarine can be launched or recovered; this is usually called a 'moon pool'. The alternative is to launch the equipment over the side but this can be restricted by poor weather conditions. An ROV is connected to the support vessel by a cable that provides the control signals and may also provide power. There is a class of ROV called an autonomous underwater vehicle (AUV) which operates without an umbilical cord or tether.

Marine research

These are specialised ships, similar to the offshore survey vessels, but they carry a much wider range of equipment and a large contingent of scientists, as well as their crew. Most of them are designed to operate in extreme cold (for Arctic and Antarctic research). They are usually from 1,000 to 3,000 tonnes displacement.

Figure 36. The Maria S Merian *in Reykjavik*

Photograph courtesy of Estermiz (CCO 1.0)

Icebreakers

Icebreakers are designed to break a path though thick ice to keep ports and sea lanes open. Icebreakers are common in Baltic and Russian ports, Chile and Canada. Their hulls are specially strengthened to allow them to crash into thick ice. Their bows are also specially designed and their propellers and rudders have to be protected from damage by ice. Some Russian icebreakers are nuclear-powered but most are diesel electric. Some ordinary merchant ships are designed to deal with ice (Ice-class ships) but these cannot match the power and strength of the true icebreaker.

Figure 37. Merchant ship escorted by a Finnish icebreaker

Figure 38. Finnish icebreaker Otso showing the icebreaking bow

Cable layers

These vessels are designed to lay and repair sub-sea cables (electric power, telephony, optical data). The first and most famous was Isambard Kingdom Brunel's vessel *Great Eastern* that laid the first successful Transatlantic cable in 1865. They have large cylindrical holds to store the coiled cable and have sheaves at bow and stern to allow the cable to pass over the deck of the ship. Some cable layers are stationed permanently at ports around the world to permit a quick response to any cable with a fault. The most modern vessels do not have a bow sheave and have additional equipment to permit other tasks offshore when they are not laying or repairing cables (see *Offshore engineering vessels*).

Figure 39. IT Intrepid

Photograph courtesy of International Telecom (www.ittelecom.com)

Salvage tugs

These vessels are a different proposition to harbour tugs. They must operate in all weathers and be able to reach a ship in distress quickly, establish a towline connection and have sufficient power to tow the disabled ship to a place of refuge. The largest salvage tugs are 6,000 DWT with engines of more than 25,000 horsepower (HP) and a towing force (bollard pull) of up to 425 tonnes. They are deployed worldwide and really earn their money when they are able to save (salvage) a vessel in distress. Salvage tugs are also used to tow very large floating objects for long distances. Most of the most modern vessels are multi-purpose and are, in effect, also offshore support vessels with specialist equipment to enable them to carry out a variety of roles.

Fishing vessels

The world deep sea fishing fleet is very large and consists of a variety of ship types from simple trawlers towing nets, through whaling vessels and up to huge factory ships which receive and refrigerate the catch whilst providing logistical support for the fishing vessels, many of which spend months at sea deployed on different fishing grounds.

Warships

Most nations with a coastline operate a naval force to protect their coast and many have larger ships that allow them to 'project' their power and influence worldwide. In international waters, these range from corvettes up to giant aircraft carriers. Warships do not have to comply with the requirements of the various International Maritime Organization (IMO) conventions, although many navies do try to comply with the conventions on pollution and personnel safety. There are between 4,000-4,500 active warships, ranging from small, armed coastal patrol craft up to huge aircraft carriers. However, many of these, although listed as active, never leave port. It is probable that fewer than 20% of these vessels are at sea at any one time.

Figure 40. The guided-missile destroyer USS Jason Dunham

Chapter 4 - Onboard ship

A ship is a microcosm of industrial activity requiring all of the support services that any small factory onshore would need, with the added complication of housing and protecting the crew and keeping the vessel seaworthy and safe. For thousands of years, this has required a hierarchical structure for the people onboard, and this structure has been adapted as ships have become more complex and undertaken longer voyages.

Organisation

The vessel is commanded by the Master, usually accorded the courtesy title of Captain. He has absolute authority onboard delegated to him by the flag State and the vessel owner. His staff and crew will be split into several departments, depending on the size and complexity of the ship. The breakdown below applies only a broad brush approach to ordinary merchant ships (tankers, dry bulk, container ships, etc.); more specialised ships will need a more complex organisational structure.

Watchkeeping

All vessels will have officers and some crew assigned to periods of duty called a watch. Watchkeeping periods are usually of four hours' duration with each watchkeeper standing two four-hour watches per day. The exceptions are warships, which have a different schedule, and some smaller vessels which operate a four hours on, four hours off schedule. The watch break down is typically as below.

Time	Bridge watch	Engine watch
00:00 – 04:00	Second Officer	Third Engineer
04:00 – 08:00	Chief Officer	Second Engineer
08:00 – 12:00	Third Officer	Fourth Engineer
12:00 – 16:00	Second Officer	Third Engineer
16:00 – 20:00	Chief Officer	Second Engineer
20:00 – 24:00	Third Officer	Fourth Engineer

The concept is that the least experienced officer is on watch whilst most of the others are awake and available. The most senior officers keep the 'twilight' watches (when the hazards are at their greatest) and the early morning and afternoon watches take place when most of the others will be asleep or working on deck.

As detailed below, on many ships the engine room is unattended for long periods (unmanned machinery space (UMS)), in which case the engineer officers will have a duty rota with each senior standing duty for a 24-hour period. When the duty engineer is not present in the engine room, all alarms are displayed in the public spaces and in the duty engineer's cabin – to which he will respond.

Deck department

This department is headed by the chief officer or 'mate' who is responsible to the Master for the navigation, cargo operations and deck maintenance. He will be assisted by other deck officers all of whom (the mate included) will usually keep a bridge watch at sea and a deck watch in port. Each of these officers will also take responsibility for certain routine tasks (navigation chart corrections, lifeboat maintenance, fire extinguisher maintenance, etc.).

Whilst on bridge watch, the officer of the watch is responsible for the safe navigation of the ship. He will be assisted by at least one other crewmember as a lookout and this will be supplemented by one or two others when navigating in restricted waters, manoeuvring or steaming in conditions of reduced visibility. In daylight and good visibility the assisting crewmember is not required to be on lookout on the bridge but can be nearby (probably engaged in maintenance duties) as long as he can be quickly recalled to the bridge if needed. The rules governing this are part of the Standards of Training, Certification and Watchkeeping (STCW) convention and there is very good guidance given in the International Chamber of Shipping's (ICS) *Bridge Procedures Guide*.

Engine department

This department is headed by the chief engineer who is responsible to the Master for all engineering tasks, maintenance and the safe operation of the machinery. He is assisted by at least two other engineer officers on most ships. On ships where the engine room is continually manned, the engineers will stand engine room watches, assisted by at least one other crewman, and on such ships the engine room department may have as many as seven officers.

On ships with extensive additional equipment for cargo care (reefer ships, cruise liners, gas carriers), there may be additional engineers to operate and maintain this equipment. Some ships also carry an electrical engineer. Most modern vessels operate with an unmanned engine room. These ships do not require engineers to stand watch on a continuous basis as the plant is very automated and only manned when entering or leaving port or when sailing in restricted waters. One engineer will act as the duty engineer, performing routine operational tasks during the day and being on standby to respond to any engine room alarms during the night. These vessels may have an engine room department of only two or three officers, depending on the size and type of ship.

Catering department

This department is headed by a chief steward assisted by at least one other steward and a cook. They are responsible for cooking and serving food and for the cleaning and organisation of the domestic accommodation onboard. On passenger vessels, this will be the largest department onboard, numbering hundreds of staff.

Manning

The size and composition of the crew on each ship is a matter for the owner. However, it must meet the minimum manning criteria laid down by the responsible flag State for each individual ship. The owner must also ensure that the staff hold the correct number and level of certificates of competency as required by the flag State. This will be regulated by the STCW convention, which covers technical knowledge and competency, work procedures, working hours' limitations and certain specialised certificates relevant to work on specific ship and cargo types. There is now a convention on the labour conditions onboard ship which came into force in 2013. Details of this can be seen in the chapter on *International Conventions*, under the section on the Maritime Labour Convention (MLC).

Training

Most flag States set standards for the training of all seafarers and this is closely integrated with the requirements of the examinations for the award of certificates of competency. These are the minimum requirements and many owners will supplement this training with additional courses that will improve the ability of their staff to operate the ships effectively and efficiently. For officers, their initial training will be a combination of study at specialised maritime colleges and at sea as an apprentice or cadet, moving on to further college time prior to sitting each certificate of competency. The ordinary crew will undertake short induction courses and simple assessments to ensure that they have the skill levels required for their departments.

Retention

Life at sea is not an easy option. In many jobs, personnel will be expected to serve onboard for periods of up to one year; the work is very hard with a very limited social life and limited entertainment. For these reasons, many seafarers give up sailing after a relatively short period, returning to shore-based employment. It is necessary for the shipowner to provide the right balance between length of tours of duty, financial reward, and work and domestic conditions onboard. If the owner gets this right, the crew will continue to work for it and it will not need to keep training replacements.

For ships' officers, in addition to the remarks above, there is also an imperative to provide a career structure, ongoing training and a degree of variety that will improve an officer's breadth of experience. It should be remembered that every officer cadet taken on enters the pool of talent from which companies will recruit their future superintendents, technical specialists and other shore-based maritime positions.

Welfare

Seafarers can spend up to a year away from their family and home. Their only support network is their fellow crew, and as crew numbers on each ship shrink, the options get fewer. Employers have a moral responsibility and some legal responsibilities over the well-being of their employees. This is not just limited to work place safety but includes health, the provision of opportunities for communication with family and friends, comfort and their security. Regrettably, there are many owners who only manage to meet the minimum legal requirements and some who do not even achieve these.

There are a few charitable organisations working in ports around the world that provide places where seafarers can find friendship, advice, support, communication facilities and other help. Most of these are faith-based but all of them welcome seafarers of all creeds. Such organisations include The Mission to Seafarers, The Marine Society and Stella Maris, but there are many others providing an oasis of support in thousands of ports worldwide.

Navigation

Deep sea navigation involves finding out exactly where you are, finding the place you want to go to, and planning and executing the voyage to reach your destination safely and efficiently.

The challenge is a very old one and, even thousands of years ago, seafarers developed techniques to undertake very long voyages out of sight of land for days at a time. Over the last few hundred years, the key tools have been the telescope (to see landmarks and obstacles), the compass (to indicate North), the chart (a map of the sea and the coast), the sextant (to measure angles) and the chronometer (for accurate determination of time).

Even today, deck officers are trained in the use of all these tools. Technology, particularly electronics, now means that with global positioning systems (GPS) based on satellite signals any ship can see its position to within a couple of metres, tell the time with great accuracy and, when integrated with electronic chart display and information systems (ECDIS), plot its position and track on electronic charts.

The modern radar allows a vessel to see landmarks, obstacles and other ships day and night from great distances. As a consequence, the old techniques are very rarely used, but if the GPS system should fail (or be switched off) then deck officers would have to revert to the old-fashioned methods. Many ships still carry paper charts, which have to be manually corrected and annotated on a routine basis (from messages and small tracings sent to each ship). However, the regulations now permit vessels to forego paper charts if they have two separate ECDIS systems. In October 2013, the United States administration announced that it was to stop producing paper charts, other than for special requests.

Ships still have a magnetic compass and a gyroscopic compass, as well as a chronometer. The one traditional instrument required every day is the telescope (or binoculars) to help with the primary task of the bridge watchkeeping officer – to keep a good visual look-out.

Careful planning of a vessel's route and close monitoring of its position, as well as the positions of other vessels which may pose a risk of collision, are the primary tasks of the bridge watchkeeping team. Many instances of collisions, groundings (where a ship touches the seabed) and wrecks can be directly attributed to defective navigation.

Traffic separation systems

When vessels are sailing in confined waters, especially where there is a lot of traffic, they may be required by the marine authority responsible for the waters to keep to a specified channel when sailing in a particular direction in order to keep ships apart. The systems used for this are called Vessel Traffic Services (VTS) and they are usually compulsory. They may force a ship to deviate from the shortest route. One of the best examples is the English Channel scheme which is jointly administered by the UK and French authorities.

Navigational marks and aids

For centuries, people have placed permanent markers and guides to help vessels to navigate difficult channels in coastal areas and rivers. Simple sticks (withies) were stuck in the sea or river bed, protruding above the water to show the recommended channel. These have now largely been replaced by floating objects called buoys, which are painted in special colours and fitted with flashing lights.

Buoyage systems

Buoys are colour and shape-coded, and are put into five categories:

Cardinal marks – these indicate where the best and safest water may be found and they are used with a compass. They show where the mariner has safe passage.

A cardinal mark may indicate.

- the deepest water in an area
- the safe side on which to pass a danger
- a particular feature in a channel, such as a bend, junction or the end of a shoal.

Lateral marks – these are usually positioned to define well-established channels and indicate port and starboard sides of the navigation route into a port.

Figure 41. New buoy   *Figure 42. Old buoy*

Photographs courtesy of Nigel Draffin

There are two sets of colour coding for lateral marks – one applies to the majority of the world (System A) and the other for the Americas, Japan, Korea and the Philippines (System B). System B reverses the colours used in System A. Put simply, it is like driving on the left or right-hand side of the road – you need to know which country you are in!

Isolated danger marks – these designate an isolated danger of limited extent that has navigable water all round it, for example an isolated shoal, rock or wreck.

Safe water marks – these indicate that there is navigable water all around a mark, for example a mid-channel or landfall buoy.

Special marks – these indicate a special area or feature, such as traffic separation marks, spoil, ground marks, cable or pipeline marks, including outfall pipes. They can also define a channel within a channel, such as a channel for deep draught ships in a wide estuary where the limits of the channel for normal navigation are marked by red and green lateral buoys.

Lighthouses

People originally used beacons or fires to provide warning of land at night. However, even as long as two thousand years ago, these began to be formalised as the tall structures we call lighthouses. Some submerged obstructions were marked by a floating lighthouse, called a lightship or lightvessel, but these have been generally replaced by large buoys.

These marks are still used today and their size, shape and colour are controlled by the International Association of Lighthouse Authorities (IALA). The marks are indicated on navigational charts and the buoyage system allows navigational channels to be clearly indicated.

Navigation lights

All ships are required to show lights at night that indicate the bow, the stern, the port side and the starboard side. Additional white lights on the mast can also indicate the type of vessel as well as its activity (special lights for fishing boats with nets out, vessels manoeuvring with difficulty, or vessels 'not under command' (or broken down)). These are referred to as navigation lights or steaming lights. A competent deck officer of the watch will be able to identify a ship, its direction of travel and any special restrictions from observing these lights.

Collision Regulations (ColRegs)

These are the rules for taking action when coming onto another ship at sea. They are laid down in the IMO International Regulations for Preventing Collisions at Sea (ColRegs) and they are incorporated in the national law of the flag State of a ship. They are much too complex to consider here but you can get some idea about them from a pamphlet published in 1867 by Thomas Gray, a senior civil servant at the British Board of Trade, called *The Rule of the Road at Sea*.

Aids to memory in four verses

1. *Two steam ships meeting*

   When both side-lights you see ahead –
   Port your helm and show your RED.

2. *Two steam ships passing*

   GREEN to GREEN – or, RED to RED –
   Perfect safety – go ahead!

3. *Two steam ships crossing*

   Note – This is the position of greatest danger; there is nothing for it but good look-out, caution and judgment.

```
If to your starboard RED appear,

It is your duty to keep clear;

To act as judgment says is proper;

To Port - or Starboard - Back - or Stop her!

But when upon your Port is seen

A Steamer's Starboard Light of GREEN,

There's not so much for you to do,

For GREEN to Port keeps clear of you.
```

4. *All ships must keep a good look-out, and steam ships must stop and go astern, if necessary.*

```
Both in safety and in doubt

Always keep a good look-out;

In danger, with no room to turn,

Ease her, Stop her, Go astern.
```

Thomas Gray, *Rule of the Road at Sea, 1867*

Gray is referring to the navigation lights of the ships described in the previous section – the light on the port side is red, the light on the starboard side is green. Unfortunately, for today's seafarer, ships now use a wheel to steer rather than a tiller, and the orders given since the late 1920s would send you the wrong way, However, the principle remains unchanged, and both ships in verse 1 should turn to starboard.

The ColRegs are much more detailed and ships' navigating lights are also much more complex but the basics remain the same.

Communication

It was at the beginning of the 20th century that ships first began to use radio communication. This communication was only in Morse code (a series of long and short sounds making up letters) and was transmitted and received by a radio officer sailing as part of the crew. By the 1950s, vessels could, when near the coast, make radio telephone calls but this was ponderous and expensive. The breakthrough came in the 1970s with telex over radio (TOR) and facsimile (fax) machines. This allowed complex messages to be communicated at reasonable cost.

As new technology developed, such as satellite communications (SATCOM) and the dedicated global maritime distress and safety system (GMDSS), the need for the dedicated radio officer disappeared and vessels could also use the Internet and e-mail. All ships use very high frequency (VHF) radio systems for talking to other ships nearby, especially in regulated traffic areas and when passing other vessels at sea. Deck officers are still required to have a working knowledge of Morse code that can be transmitted by a signalling lamp or Aldis lamp that all ships carry. Whilst this technique is actively employed on warships, it is very seldom used on merchant ships.

Safety onboard

All merchant vessels must have appropriate life-saving appliances onboard as required by international convention and the requirements of their flag State. There must be sufficient lifeboats and, if the vessel has a free fall lifeboat at the stern, there must also be a rescue boat that can be launched by gravity.

Figure 43. Free fall lifeboat

Photograph courtesy of Trevor Harrison

The vessel must have effective fire-fighting systems (both portable and fixed installations) and most ships also must carry self-contained breathing apparatus. Tankers have strict requirements for tank entry, with test equipment to ensure that any space to be entered has a safe atmosphere with regard to flammable gas levels, oxygen levels, toxic gas detection, etc. Many other ships carry this equipment as a matter of company policy.

A recent problem is piracy at sea. Many vessels are equipped with non-lethal deterrents to prevent pirates from boarding, and they may also have a citadel where the crew can take shelter and await rescue. There are commercial professional security services that are contracted to sail onboard vessels in transit though high-risk areas. Such a service depends on the rules of the flag State which will determine if the security team can carry weapons and under what circumstances they may use lethal force. This is a problematic area for shipowners.

Mooring

When a vessel has to come to a berth alongside in a port, either to berth alongside another ship or tie up at a buoy in a port or at an offshore location, she will need to 'moor', using ropes or wires to secure her.

The mooring ropes or wires are tensioned using winches fitted onto the deck of the ship. A similar (but more powerful) device, called a windlass, is used to raise and lower the anchors that 'anchor' the ship to the seabed in an 'anchorage'.

Figure 44. A combined winch and windlass on the forecastle of a tanker

Photograph courtesy of Rolls-Royce (www.rolls-royce.com)

The diagram below shows the use of mooring lines.

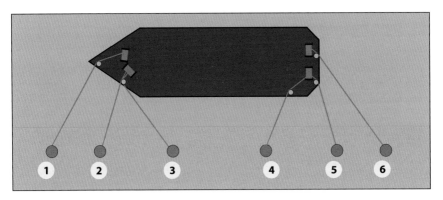

Figure 45. Mooring ropes

Diagram courtesy of Petrospot

Number	Name	Purpose
1	Bow line	Prevent backwards movement
2	Forward breast line	Keep close to pier
3	After bow spring line	Prevent from advancing
4	Forward quarter spring line	Prevent from moving back
5	Quarter breast line	Keep close to pier
6	Stern line	Prevent forwards movement

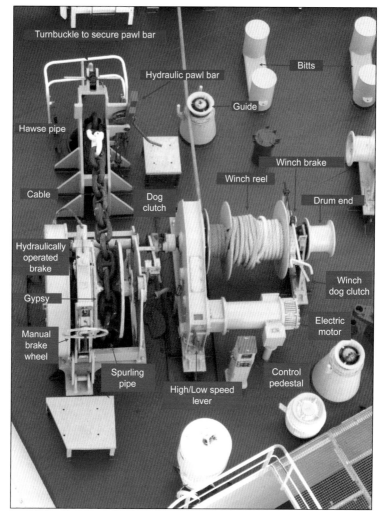

Figure 46. The elements of a combined winch-windlass

Photograph courtesy of Welkinridge

Anchoring

When a vessel needs to be held at a particular location 'at sea' where there is no facility to moor to a fixed structure or a special buoy it will use its anchors. These are very large and heavy structures attached to the ship by an anchor chain (or anchor cable). The anchor chain actually weighs considerably more than the anchor. The windlass used to raise the anchor is specially designed to grip the links in the anchor chain. Most deep sea ships will have sufficient chain to allow them to anchor in 200 m depth of water. The anchor is designed to dig itself into the seabed when placed under strain, but the watchkeepers must always monitor the ship's position to be sure that the anchor is holding firm. If it is not, the ship can be said to be dragging its anchor. The nature of the seabed is important in helping the anchor to hold, and anchorages are chosen to maximise the holding effect as well as providing sheltered water.

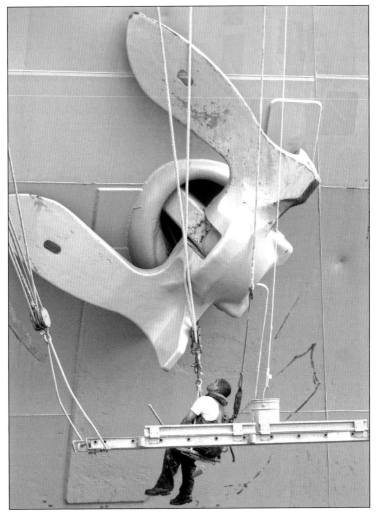

Figure 47. 20-tonne anchor in the anchor pocket on a warship

Photograph courtesy of the US Navy

Bow thrusters

Most vessels will require the assistance of tugs when berthing in a port. When a vessel is moving slowly through the water, the effectiveness of the rudder is much reduced and, as a consequence, modern vessels are often fitted with bow thrusters (and sometimes stern thrusters) that can push the ship sideways, thereby assisting the tugs or, on some ships, replacing them.

These thrusters are large ducts running from one side of the hull below the waterline to the other side, each containing an electrically-powered, reversible propeller. This allows water to be directed from one side of the hull to the other and will help the ship to manoeuvre at slow speed. It also reduces the amount of assistance needed from tugs.

Chapter 5 - Classification and insurance

Every vessel in international trade needs to have insurance to cover the cost of claims made for damage by third parties. This is provided by Protection and Indemnity (P&I) clubs and without this cover a ship will not be allowed into many ports and very few charterers will fix the vessel to carry a cargo. The owner may also choose to have insurance to cover damage to its own vessel in the form of hull and machinery insurance. This is not compulsory and the cover will be arranged, if required, though marine insurers. In order to get insurance cover, the owner must demonstrate that the ship has been built and has been inspected for compliance with rules set by a classification (class) society. These societies publish rules for construction which are aligned with the minimum requirements of the relevant IMO conventions but which will exceed these requirements and cover significantly more detail than required by the IMO.

Classification societies

The early insurers of ships (usually merchants with sufficient finance) would insure or underwrite the risk of a voyage with a number taking a proportion of the risk of each voyage. They realised that they needed a way to assess the condition of the ship they were underwriting and, in 1760, they set up the Register Society, later renamed as Lloyd's Register of Ships. A simple code was then developed to identify if a ship was well built and, in good condition; from this we derived the expression that a ship was 'A1 at Lloyd's' (best construction and in sound condition).

The class societies have rules on the construction of ships to which a vessel must adhere if it is to be classed by them. The rules are not all identical but all will meet the minimal requirements of the IMO, and each society has its own 'additions' for matters such as unmanned engine room operation, enhanced safety, enhanced environmental protection, etc.

The most significant 'add on' is Ice Class, which determines under what conditions and with what help a ship can sail in waters restricted by International Navigation Limits (see the section on *Restrictions on Insurance*). For example, the American Bureau of Shipping (ABS) Ice Class goes from A5 to D0. This covers those vessels which can sail unescorted in Polar regions (with at least a 60% reduction in insurance premiums) down to vessels which have very specific restrictions but which can sail in some parts of the Baltic Sea during the ice season on payment of the full insurance premium.

The Ice Class rules call for additional hull strengthening, protection of propellers and sea water intakes and, for class A5 or equivalent, many other special requirements.

Lloyd's Register was followed by the establishment of societies in other countries, including France, Norway, Italy, Germany and Japan. There are now at least 50 of them but only 13 are in the group which is generally accepted as the top level, the International Association of Classification Societies (IACS). The table below shows a selection.

Classification societies

Society	Abbreviation	Founded	Office	IACS member
Lloyd's Register	LR	1760	London	Yes
Bureau Veritas	BV	1828	Paris	Yes
Registro Italiano Navale	RINA	1861	Genoa	Yes
American Bureau of Shipping	ABS	1862	Houston	Yes
Det Norske Veritas*	DNV	1864	Oslo	Yes
Germanischer Lloyd*	GL	1867	Hamburg	Yes
Nippon Kaiji Kyokai (ClassNK)	NK	1899	Tokyo	Yes
Russian Maritime Register of Shipping	RS	1913	Saint Petersburg	Yes
Hellenic Register of Shipping	HR	1919	Piraeus	No
Polish Register of Shipping	PRS	1936	Gdansk	Yes
Croatian Register of Shipping	CRS	1949	Split	Yes
Bulgarian Register of Shipping	BRS	1950	Varna	No
China Corporation Register of Shipping	CR	1951	Taipei	No
China Classification Society	CCS	1956	Beijing	Yes
Korean Register of Shipping	KR	1960	Busan	Yes
Turk Loydu	TL	1962	Istanbul	No
Registro Internacional Naval	RINAVE	1973	Lisbon	No

Indian Register of Shipping	IRS	1975	Mumbai	Yes
International Naval Surveys Bureau	INSB	1977	Piraeus	No
Brazilian Register of Shipping	RBNA	1982	Rio de Janeiro	No
International Register of Shipping	IROS	1993	Miami	No
Ships Classification Malaysia	SCM	1994	Shah Alam	No
Isthmus Bureau of Shipping	IBS	1995	Panama	No
Guardian Bureau of Shipping	GBS	1996	Syria	No
Shipping Register of Ukraine	RU	1998	Kyiv	No
Dromon Bureau of Shipping	DBS	2003	Limassol	No
Overseas Marine Certification Services	OMCS	2004	Panama	No
Intermaritime Certification Services	ICS Class	2005	Panama	No
Venezuelan Register of Shipping	VRS	2008	London	No

* In 2012, DNV and GL signed an agreement to merge. The new entity is known as DNV GL Group.

All these societies have their own rules and, for legal reasons, the only certification they will give is that a vessel is in compliance with their specific rules according to the notation on the certificate. They employ teams of engineers and naval architects who check yard designs, attend the shipbuilding yards and visit ships in service to ensure that the class is maintained. The societies provide other services, such as issuing and auditing certificates of compliance with various voluntary codes (such as International Organization for Standardization (ISO) 9000, ISO 1400, etc.) on behalf of shipowners, and approving and auditing some statutory codes (such as ISM) on behalf of some flag States.

Marine insurance

Hull and machinery insurance is purchased by vessel owners from the commercial market. The insurer will not usually insure a vessel unless it is 'in class'. There will also be insurance in place on the cargo. The shipowner is usually able to limit any liability for the value of the cargo in accordance with the rules of the particular contract of carriage (Hague Rules, Hamburg Rules, etc.) but this limitation only applies as long as the ship is seaworthy. Should a vessel cease to be 'in class', this will affect the owner's ability to show the ship is seaworthy.

There are two ways in which an owner can influence the cost of insurance (beyond the age of the ship and the hull value). One is to accept a proportion of any claim for its own account (the deductible). Depending on the owner's financial position, this could be as small as $50,000 or as much as $500,000. The other alternative is to forego hull and machinery cover – if an owner can stand the financial loss of the asset and the vessel is old (with a low hull value and a high premium) this may make good financial sense.

Protection and Indemnity (P&I) clubs

These are mutual societies of shipowners which maintain a pool of funds to meet an insured liability from one of their members. The first was the Shipowners Mutual in 1855 and there are now 13 members of the International Group of P&I Clubs that represent 90% of oceangoing tonnage.

There are no shareholders in a club, only club members. They pay an annual subscription (a call) and if the pool fund is becoming depleted, there may be an additional 'call' on all members. Their purpose is to protect the members from claims that cannot be covered by conventional insurance and the number of countries demanding that vessels entering their ports have valid P&I cover is increasing. This is linked to vessels being able to show sufficient cover to meet the Civil Liabilities Convention (CLC) and the Bunker Convention. Similar separate requirements exist for all tankers.

The list below shows the members of the International Group of P&I Clubs:

American Steamship Owners Mutual Protection and Indemnity Association Inc.

Assuranceforeningen Skuld

Gard P&I (Bermuda) Ltd

The Britannia Steam Ship Insurance Association Ltd

The Japan Ship Owners' Mutual Protection & Indemnity Association

The London Steam-Ship Owners' Mutual Insurance Association Ltd

The North of England Protection & Indemnity Association Ltd

The Shipowners' Mutual Protection & Indemnity Association (Luxembourg)

The Standard Club Ltd

The Steamship Mutual Underwriting Association (Bermuda) Ltd

The Swedish Club

United Kingdom Mutual Steam Ship Assurance Association (Bermuda) Ltd

The West of England Ship Owners Mutual Insurance Association (Luxembourg)

Restrictions on insurance

There are two important restrictions on insurance cover – one is 'war risks', which is self-explanatory (the 'risk' areas are determined by the Joint War Risk Committee), and the other is often referred to as 'institute warranty limits' (but should now be called 'international navigation limits' (by the Joint Hull Committee Navigating Limits sub-committee)), which declares that certain areas are at a permanent or seasonal risk of ice damage. The restrictions are determined and imposed by committees of the Lloyd's Market Association (LMA), and it is then up to the insurers to offer cover for additional premium if they so wish.

General Average

When Phoenecian traders were tramping around the Mediterranean Sea thousands of years ago, it was common for the cargo owners to travel on the ship. If a vessel was caught in a severe storm, it might be necessary to jettison (throw overboard) some of the cargo to save the ship. Not unnaturally, the owner of that part of the cargo could be aggrieved and so a mechanism was sought to 'share the burden of loss'. This became known as General Average, where one party to the adventure which sacrificed its position could seek compensation from all the other parties involved. General Average can be found in all charter parties and is included in the insurance cover. It is written into the rules covering the contract of carriage (the Hague Rules, etc.).

Chapter 6 - International conventions

For almost all maritime matters, international conventions are proposed, debated and established by the IMO through its committee structures and national delegations. These conventions, once established, have to be ratified by member states and, once a convention has been ratified by a pre-agreed percentage of nations and/or a pre-agreed percentage of gross tonnage of ships flagged by those member states that have ratified, then it will enter into force. The members who have ratified need to translate the convention into their national laws before they can enforce the provisions of the convention on their ships (flag State) and in their ports (port State).

International Maritime Organization (IMO)

The IMO is part of the United Nations (UN) and is headquartered in London. It was founded in 1948 as the Inter-Governmental Maritime Consultative Organization (IMCO) but its name was changed in 1959 to the IMO.

It has 170 member states and three associate members. It works through a series of committees and sub-committees, each with working groups, correspondence groups and drafting groups. Whilst the delegations are drawn from the national members, there are a number of non-governmental organisations (NGOs) that have been granted consultative status. These include most maritime trade and industry associations (the International Chamber of Shipping (ICS), INTERTANKO, INTERCARGO, the Society for International Gas Tankers and Terminal Operators (SIGTTO), the International Bunker Industry Association (IBIA), the Institute of Marine Engineering, Science and Technology (IMarEST), and the Baltic and International Maritime Council (BIMCO), etc.). These 80 NGOs provide the technical breadth and depth to the discussions and they participate in the groups but have no vote. The IMO is often criticised for taking too long to make changes but it must be remembered that it is operated by consensus and the need to persuade its members can be a complex, time consuming and sometimes political process.

Safety of Life at Sea (SOLAS)

SOLAS was the first convention to come out of the IMO in 1960. It built on the work of the first conference after the loss of the *Titanic* (SOLAS 1914), the 1929 conference (SOLAS 1929), and the first IMCO conference (SOLAS 1948). The original IMO convention (SOLAS 1960) has since been completely rewritten (SOLAS 1974) and has been subject to many amendments since then. It is the cornerstone of ship safety, covering navigation, ship construction, certification, life-saving appliances and many other issues.

Marine Pollution (MARPOL)

The MARPOL convention came from the OILPOL convention of 1954 that was set up by a separate conference. It was agreed that responsibility for this area would pass to the IMO when it became fully functioning, and the result was MARPOL 1973. This convention did not achieve the required number of signatories and, as a consequence, was further amended in 1978 by a special protocol. It is often referred to as MARPOL 73/78.

It entered into force in 1983 and has been amended many times to cover vessel pollution from many sources (garbage, air pollution, paint, ballast water and scrubber effluent). MARPOL impacts shipping in many areas, especially double-hulled tankers and sulphur oxide (SOx) rules for fuel (see the section on *Pollution* for more details).

Standards of Training, Certification and Watchkeeping (STCW)

This convention was adopted in 1978 and subsequently amended in 1995 and 2008. It sets out basic requirements on training, certification and watchkeeping for seafarers on an international level. It also sets out minimum standards for the training, assessment and certification for all seafarers, including supplementary certification for gas ships, dynamic positioning, operations in Polar regions as well as requirements for training to use new technology, such as ECDIS and GMDSS.

Maritime Labour Convention (MLC)

This convention was signed in 2006 under the auspices of the International Labour Organization (ILO), which is a part of the UN tasked with dealing with labour issues. It reached the required number of ratifications in 2012, entering into force in 2013. It lays down minimum standards as follows:

Minimum requirements for seafarers to work on a ship

- Age
- Fitness
- Training
- Recruitment

Employment conditions

- Contracts
- Payments

- Rest hours
- Leave
- Repatriation
- Loss of ship
- Manning

Accommodation, recreational facilities, food and catering

- Accommodation
- Food and catering

Health protection, medical care, welfare and social security protection

- Medical care onboard ship and ashore
- Shipowners' liability
- Health and safety protection and accident prevention
- Access to shore-based welfare facilities
- Social security

Compliance and enforcement

- Flag States
- Port States
- Labour agencies.

United Nations Convention on the Law of the Sea (UNCLOS)

This convention deals with territorial waters, sub-sea mineral rights and a number of other similar issues. It defines what is meant by a harbour and lays down the right to transit territorial waters, known as 'the right of innocent passage'.

Chapter 7 - National law

In general, there is no such thing as 'international law'. Instead, we have international conventions which are translated into national law in the countries which sign or ratify the original convention or, if that convention has already entered into force, then new countries will accede to the convention. Once they have done this, they then have the power to enforce the provisions of the convention.

Flag States

Every ship in international trade has to be registered with a nation state with a shipping register. The ship will fly the flag of that state and be registered in a port in that state. That state is then the flag State for the ship and responsible for ensuring the ship complies with national law in respect of all maritime legislation. Many traditional shipping nation states have an international registry that allows them to compete on costs with those registries that may be in small shipping countries with big commercially attractive registers. There are often different rules, especially on manning, between a nation's traditional registry and its 'international' registry. Ship registries can generate considerable income for a nation.

Port States

The policing of international conventions is a two-tier system. The primary responsibility is with the flag State, but not only may the flag State be geographically distant from the area where a ship operates but many flag States do not have the resources to police their fleets. The IMO conventions make provision for a second level of control, the port State; this is the state in whose port a vessel calls. The maritime authorities in that state have the right to inspect any ship entering their ports and to check for compliance with any and all relevant conventions – this is called Port State Control (PSC). The national law of that country will enable them to impose penalties for any breach of a convention, even if the breach occurred elsewhere.

The IMO originally intended that the flag State should be the principal control but over the last 30 years it is the port State that has carried out most of the checks and imposed most of the penalties.

Memoranda of Understanding (MoU)

Given the involvement of port State control in policing the conventions, it became clear that there was an opportunity for port States to coordinate their actions and keep statistics on the number of ships inspected and the incidence of noncompliance. The IMO encouraged the creation of regional port State control organisations and they are arranged and operated though Memoranda of Understanding (MoU). To date, there are nine; the United States does not directly contribute but operates an information exchange with the other regions.

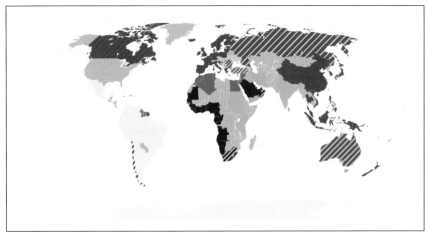

Figure 48. Memoranda of understanding

Picture courtesy of Kristofferjay (CC BY-SA 3.0)

Area	Colour
Paris MoU	Blue
Tokyo MoU	Red
Indian Ocean MoU	Green
Mediterranean MoU	Dark green
Acuerdo Latino	Yellow
Caribbean MoU	Olive
Abuja MoU	Dark red
Black Sea MoU	Cyan
Riyadh MoU	Navy

Countries with stripes are members of more than one MoU.

Chapter 8 - Ports

Ports are industrial areas equipped to receive vessels for the purpose of loading or discharging cargo, repairs, receiving stores and supplies. They are regulated by a combination of national and local legislation and they vary enormously in character. The operations they undertake can be determined by their geography and size, as well as the mix of vessel types making calls. Some ports are situated in a river estuary or further upstream. Other ports may be restricted by tides, with some or all berths being only accessible at certain stages of the tide – small ports may accommodate vessels which sit on the bottom whilst the tide is 'out', leading to the expression in a charter 'always afloat or safely aground'. There are many ports, including some very large ones, where the main area is within a basin and can only be accessed by passing through locks (the Port of Antwerp, for example). This can restrict access to certain tidal conditions but it does mean that the draught alongside the quays is constant, no matter what the state of the tide is outside the lock.

Port administration

The management of the port will come under the control of a port manager who may also be the harbour master. He will oversee a large staff which will deal with the bureaucracy of the port business and manage the logistics. In some ports, the infrastructure is wholly owned by the port management. In others, there are privately owned and controlled terminals and facilities, but they are still under the oversight of the manager of the port.

The harbour master has the right to regulate the time and manner of access; in other words, he can delay or recognise arrival or departure as required as long as it does not endanger safety. He also has the right to refuse entry if he considers a vessel poses a danger to people or the environment.

The port authorities have to be advised of a number of specific items prior to the entry of a vessel into a port, such as the mandatory information reports required by international conventions (ship security status, hazardous cargo declarations, etc.). Usually, this information is communicated to the port administration by a vessel's agent in the port. However, for vessels in certain short sea trades and those of companies with very regular calls in the port, the owner may choose to communicate this information directly between the vessel and the port administration.

The port administration will usually be responsible for the navigational aids in the port, the dredging and marking of navigational areas and the rules on the safe conduct of navigation (if tugs are required, how many tugs for each ship, speed restrictions and managing the flow of vessel traffic to ensure the safety of all vessels in the port). If there is a vessel traffic service (VTS) in the port, this will be operated by the port administration. The port will also have to survey the port quays and any underwater obstacles to ensure that charts, channel markers and buoys are correctly placed and recorded.

Pilots

Harbour pilots are professional seafarers who have undertaken additional training and detailed familiarisation with the port in which they operate. Their function is to provide local advice on the tidal streams, currents, obstacles and obstructions which may be hazardous to navigation in the port to the Masters of ships entering, berthing and leaving the port.

The Master will, in almost all cases, be in command of the ship even with the pilot onboard (the typical entry in a ship's log book is: 'Master's command, pilot's advice'). The ship is responsible for employing the pilot and paying for his services, although he will usually be engaged by the ship's agent.

Smaller vessels, especially those where the Master has considerable experience of navigating in the port, may be granted a pilotage exemption certificate. The pilot will board a ship before she enters the harbour and, when taking a ship out of port, he will leave once she has cleared the harbour. The pilot is usually transported by a pilot launch and then has to make a difficult transition from the launch and climb up the ship's side by ladder. In large ports, such as the Port of Rotterdam, the pilot frequently boards the ship by helicopter.

Pilots are also used for some transits of restricted waters, such as the English Channel, the Great Barrier Reef in Australia and the Great Belt in Denmark. In most of these areas, pilotage is not compulsory for a vessel in transit but owners and operators are strongly recommended to take a pilot due to the congested and difficult nature of the waterways.

Figure 49. Pilot boarding ship

Port dues

Any ship calling at a port has to pay various dues and levies to the port authorities that are put towards the costs of running the port and maintaining the publicly-owned infrastructure. The dues are usually based on the net tonnage of the vessel, and there may also be charges based on the actual quantity and type of cargo loaded or discharged.

Agents

Vessel owners will usually engage the services of a ship's agent as their representative whilst the vessel is in port. The agent will arrange the various documentation formalities prior to port entry, and book the pilots and any shore-based workers required for berthing and unberthing, as well act as liaison between the ship and others for all of the activities in the port. A ship's agent ensures that everything the ship needs in port (stores, fuel, new crew) arrives on time. The agent is paid an agency fee by the owner and will invoice for additional costs incurred, presenting the owner with a 'disbursement account' detailing all the transactions.

Port infrastructure

A working port needs a lot of real estate and a lot of equipment. There will be wharves or quays alongside which the vessel will moor to work cargo. The wharves may need large cranes, both fixed and mobile, for shifting cargo. Cargo receivers need warehouses to store the cargo prior to loading and after discharge. If the wharf is privately owned then the owner will charge wharfage for use of the quay.

Cranes

The most visible assets in a main port are the container cranes. These have to be high enough and wide enough to service the biggest container ships.

Figure 50. Ship and cranes in harbour, Rotterdam

Bulk terminals need special cranes with giant grabs for unloading ships and conveyor belts for loading them. Grain cargo is frequently handled by huge pneumatic suction elevators which are used to unload the ships.

Oil terminal flow booms

At quays designed for loading and discharging liquid cargo, the ship is connected to shore pipelines via hoses suspended on a special gantry or by large articulated pipes called flow booms. Oil terminals in a port are usually situated some distance from the normal cargo wharves for safety reasons. Fig. 52 shows the use of flow booms.

Figure 51. Grain transfer from ship to shore

Photograph courtesy of The Bühler Group (www.buhlergroup.com)

Figure 52. Vopak Westpoort terminal

Photograph courtesy of Vopak (www.vopak.com)

Product tankers normally use gantries of flexible hoses for loading and discharging.

Figure 53. Product tanker terminal

Photograph courtesy of Nigel Draffin

The largest tankers also require a lot of space to manoeuvre in port so their terminals are usually situated near to the port entrance. Tankers also load at offshore loading and discharging buoys, either a set of four buoys anchored to the seabed (a conventional buoy mooring) or a special rotating buoy called a single buoy mooring (SBM) or a single point mooring (SPM). These latter two types allow the tanker to rotate around the buoy as the tide and wind change – this is called weather vaneing. The cargo connection is via large floating hoses connected to the buoy which then has a drop line to an undersea pipeline which links it to the shore.

Figure 54. Very large crude carrier (VLCC)

Photograph courtesy of Nigel Draffin

Bunkering

Most ships will take on fuel in port. This fuel is called 'bunkers' and is supplied by pipeline, by road tank wagon (RTW) or, most often, by bunker barges (small tankers). The port will have regulations to regulate where and when this activity can take place. For safety reasons, it is common to restrict bunkering to certain quays or to anchorages inside the port. There may also be restrictions on bunkering at night. The value of bunker fuel is very high – often estimated to represent 50%-80% of the ship's operating costs – and efficient and safe transfer of the fuel to the ship is very important. Many ports have detailed regulations and procedures to govern bunkering activities.

Offshore bunkering

Ships sometimes engage in voyages to and from ports where there are no bunkers available. While this can be remedied by making a 'bunker only call' (entering an intermediate port just for the purpose of replenishing fuel), there is another solution. It is possible to rendezvous with a bunker supply tanker and receive fuel at sea. This may be done with both ships at anchor, both ships drifting or even with both ships underway. This is common for merchant vessels working out of West African ports or loading cargo at offshore loading facilities. Most large fishing vessels and many offshore survey ships take much of their fuel in this way.

Warships regularly replenish fuel at sea from specialist tankers and this transfer is done with the vessels steaming side-by-side but not linked by anything more than the bunker hose. This operation is called 'replenishment at sea' (RAS).

Figure 55. USS Carl Vinson *Battle Group conducts a replenishment at sea (RAS) in the Western Pacific Ocean*

Photograph courtesy of US Navy (Photographer: Dustin Howell)

Chandlers

Ship chandlers provide all the stores a vessel needs, ranging from food to linen and brushes to toilet paper. They will also provide a number of general mechanical components but they do not usually provide spare parts for the engine room. A ship will submit a requirement via the ship's agent before arrival and the chandler will deliver it during the port stay.

Water

Most modern vessels can produce fresh water and drinking water onboard using distillation plants, or so-called reverse osmosis plants. Ships without this facility will need to load fresh water in port. Ships that usually produce their own water may still find it economical to lift additional fresh water in port. The water is supplied by RTW or by barge.

Repairs

Most ships will carry out major repairs in port, either alongside berth or in a dry dock. Most repairs alongside can be completed in less than 24 hours but a vessel will need permission for immobilisation from the port authority, as it cannot be moved quickly in case of fire or accident.

Dry docks

Longer repairs or repairs that require access to the parts of the ship usually underwater will generally be carried out in a dry dock. A traditional dry dock is a U-shaped berth where the open end can be sealed off from the sea once the vessel is berthed inside. The water is then pumped out and the ship rests on special supports while the repairs are done. This is also referred to as a 'graving dock'.

There is also a type of repair facility called a 'synchrolift' or a 'ship lift', where the vessel is manoeuvred over a submerged platform which is then lifted up underneath the hull of the ship, until the entire ship is above the water level. Synchrolift docks are limited by their lifting capacity, the largest being capable of lifting 25,000 tonnes.

Conventional dry docks are also limited by the dimensions of the enclosed space. At the time of writing, the largest dry dock is in Belfast which, with a length of 556 m and a breadth of 93 m, is served by two gantry cranes, each capable of lifting 840 tonnes. There are also fixed portal cranes in a Chinese yard that can lift blocks of 20,000 tonnes and these are used to construct oil rigs.

Figure 56. Graving dock

Photograph courtesy of Nigel Draffin

Figure 57. Flooding a graving dock after painting the hull of the USS Kearsage

Photograph courtesy of the US Navy

Figure 58. Fishing vessel on the Cape Town synchrolift dock

Photograph courtesy of Nigel Draffin

Port vessels

All ports are served by a variety of smaller vessels engaged in supplying liquids such as fuel and water, discharging or loading smaller parcels of bulk cargo (barges), berthing the ships (harbour tugs) or ferrying dock workers and mooring lines (workboats).

Barges

Barges working in ports can range in size from 250 DWT up to well over 10,000 DWT. Some are used for the carriage of dry bulk cargo, some for water and others for delivering bulk fuel or lubricating oil. Their design varies from port to port but most are self powered and those carrying liquids will have their own pumps. The exception is in the United States where most barges have no propulsion but are moved from quay to ship by tugs.

Figure 59. Bunker barge

Photograph courtesy of Nigel Draffin

Tugs

Harbour tugs come in all shapes and sizes. Most modern tugs are called tractor tugs and have azimuthing thrusters. These are propellers beneath the hull that can be rotated to thrust in any direction, giving them the same pulling or pushing power in any direction they need to push. More traditional tugs still have complex nozzles arranged around their propellers to direct the propeller thrust and they will also have a very large rudder area for their size. These tugs do not need to sail quickly but they must be able to develop a thrust (bollard pull) large enough to move ships very much larger than they are.

Figure 60. Tug

Photograph courtesy of Nigel Draffin

Workboats

These are small boats used to carry mooring lines from a ship to the shore, ferry dock workers from quay to quay, as well as transport surveyors, agents, port officials and pilots. Their size and design will vary according to their function; pilot boats need to be fast and to have good sea-keeping qualities to get the pilot out to a ship at the port entrance in bad weather.

Ports may have other floating assets, such as floating docks (for ship repair) and floating cranes for cargo loading and discharge, especially of project cargo. They will also have dredgers to keep the navigable channels clear to the required depth.

Dredger

A dredger is a vessel designed to lift spoil (sand, mud, stones, etc.) from the seabed in order to create or maintain a channel for safe navigation. There are many types, with chains of buckets, with single large crane-operated grabs and, as shown in Fig. 61, with large pipes trailing over the side of the dredger to suck up the spoil. Some dredgers are very big – the *Leiv Eiriksson* is a trailing hopper dredger of 223 m in length which is able to dredge to a depth of 150 m and carry 46,000 m^3 of spoil.

Figure 61. Trailing suction dredger Geopotes 14

Floating dock

This is a dry dock that can be ballasted down to allow a ship to sail on to it. The ballast water is then pumped out, lifting the ship above the level of the water to permit repairs to be undertaken. A floating dock can be moved from port to port.

Figure 62. Barge/container carrier in floating dry dock at Hamburg

Floating crane

This is a crane mounted on a barge. The smallest floating crane has a lifting capacity of 50 to 100 tonnes and such cranes are frequently used for lifting containers from small feeder ships that would otherwise have to occupy a container berth and require the use of one of the main container cranes. They are a very common sight in Hong Kong harbour. The largest floating cranes can lift thousands of tonnes and are used in ship salvage and project and construction work.

Figure 63. Big floating crane

Photograph courtesy of Nigel Draffin

The largest floating cranes will only be found in ports with large shipyards and they have to be capable of making long ocean transits, towed by tugs to reach the sites where they are required to work. They will be involved in port construction, oil field platform installation and salvage work.

Figure 64. Giant floating crane in Japan

Locks

There are times when the water level in a seaway or river is lower than the level in a basin or canal. In order to shift a vessel from one to the other, it is necessary to use a lock or a series of locks to lift the vessel up or to let it down. Locks have been used since the Middle Ages and their operational capabilities are limited only by the size of vessel they can enclose and the absolute difference in the water level. The largest locks are on the Panama Canal.

Fig. 65 shows the sequence for a small boat entering a canal lock to rise up to a new level and for a small boat to enter a lock to be lowered down one level.

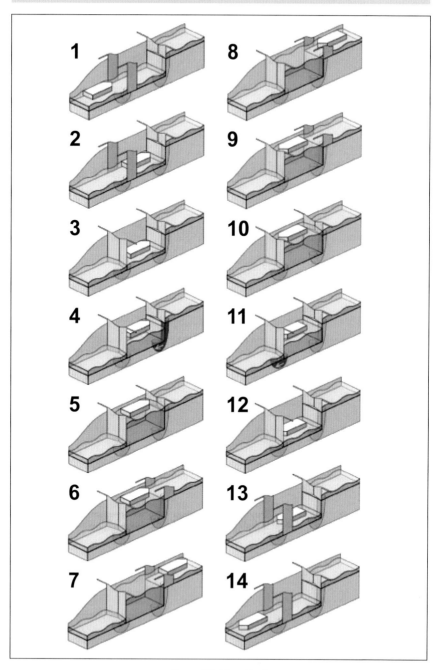

Figure 65. Canal lock

1.   Boat sailing upstream

2.   Boat enters lock

3.   Downstream gates close

4/5.   Chamber filled

6.   Upstream gates open

7.   Boat leaves lock

8.   Boat sailing downstream

9.   Boat enters lock

10.   Upstream gates close

11/12. Chamber emptied

13.   Downstream gates open

14.   Boat leaves lock.

Chapter 9 - Canals

Canals are man-made waterways and have been used for thousands of years. They provide a seaway for ships where there is no natural route. The largest canals are amongst the biggest engineering projects ever undertaken and the effort that goes into their construction and maintenance reflects the savings they make in terms of vessel time.

Suez Canal

The Suez Canal is the oldest very large canal and connects the Red Sea to the Mediterranean. It was built in 1869 by Ferdinand de Lesseps (he had some help!). The canal can accept vessels of 40 m beam and with a draught of 19 m (a VLCC in ballast, a part-loaded VLCC or a fully-loaded Suezmax tanker). The vessels transit the canal in convoys: two convoys southbound and one northbound each day. The convoys pass in a man-made bypass and a natural passing place called the Great Bitter Lakes. The second southbound convoy is made up of smaller ships because of the limitations of the man-made bypass. There are no locks on the Suez Canal.

Figure 66. Container ship Hanjin Kaohsiung *in transit*

Photograph courtesy of Daniel Csörföly

Figure 67. USS Dwight D Eisenhower *aircraft carrier transiting the Suez Canal*

Panama Canal

The Panama Canal was completed in 1914 and connects the Caribbean with the Pacific Ocean. The canal has three sets of locks, one on the Caribbean side and two on the Pacific side. The vessels transit the locks in convoys and the maximum size is determined by the dimensions of the locks. At present, vessels are limited to a beam of 32.3 m, a length of 296 m and a draught of 12.6 m, and this gives us the ship definition 'Panamax'.

The locks on the Panama canal are as follows:

The lock chambers are 110 ft (33.53 m) wide by 1,050 ft (320 m) long, with a usable length of 1,000 ft (305 m). The total lift (the amount by which a ship is raised or lowered) in the three steps of the Gatun locks is 85 ft (25.9 m); the lift of the two-step Miraflores locks is 54 ft (16 m). The single-step Pedro Miguel locks have a lift of 31 ft (9.4 m). The lift at Miraflores actually varies due to the extreme tides on the Pacific side, between 43 ft (13 m) at extreme high tide and 64.5 ft (20 m) at extreme low tide. The tidal differences on the Atlantic side are very small.

The Panama Canal Authority wants to increase the maximum ship size to a beam of 49 m, a length of 365 m and a draught of 15 m. The expansion project will include building new locks at each end of the Canal and carrying out other works to increase the maximum size of vessel which can transit the Canal (this size is known as New Panamax). The new lock chambers are 180 feet (ft) (54.86 m) wide by 1,400 ft (426.72 m) long, with a usable length of about 1,200 ft (365 m). The new locks are in parallel to the original ones.

Work on the expansion programme is scheduled for completion in 2015/2016.

Figure 68. Miraflores locks on the Panama Canal

Figure 69. Ro-Ro Tourcoing *transiting Miraflores locks*

Photograph courtesy of Dozenist (CC BY-SA 3.0)

Kiel Canal

The Kiel Canal connects the North Sea, via the lower reaches of the River Elbe, to the Baltic Sea. The maximum size is limited to a beam of 32.5 m, a length of 235 m and a draft of 9.5 m. The canal has locks at each end.

Figure 70. Container ship Anna Sirkka entering the Kiel Canal

Photograph courtesy of Robert Cutts (CC BY-SA 2.0)

Figure 71. Kiel Canal

Chapter 10 - Making money

Merchant ships exist to make money. Each sector has its own way of calculating voyage costs and charging for service and there is no 'one size fits all'. The first man with a boat capable of crossing a river would have offered to carry passengers or goods for barter of goods or another 'service' from his passengers. The ferryman would have regarded the cost of building and maintaining his craft and the use of his own time as the necessary overheads of his business. Little has changed, except that the use of barter, whilst still practised, is comparatively rare.

As vessels became larger, the investments bigger, the manpower required greater and the voyages more complex, a system evolved that allowed the use of more efficient payment and reward.

Chartering

A charter arrangement is a contract between the entity which controls the ship (the 'disponent owner') and the entity which requires the service to carry cargo or passengers. This arrangement is often called a 'charter party' and will detail the exact conditions of the contract. The disponent owner is often not the owner of the ship and the entity entering into the charter is not always the owner of the cargo.

Voyage chartering

A voyage charter is an agreement to carry a quantity of cargo of a particular type from port A to port B for an agreed cost. The charterer takes no part in the actual operation of the voyage other than to arrange for the cargo to be delivered to the ship at port A and to receive the cargo at port B. It is the equivalent of taking a taxi journey. The biggest complications come where the cargo is not the only cargo onboard or where the exact ports are not known before the commencement of the charter. Different shipping sectors have evolved methods to overcome these complications. In the case of tankers, this can involve the use of the Worldwide Tanker Nominal Freight Scale (Worldscale), and for dry bulk, the use of a trip time charter.

In Appendix 3 to this book, the first page provides the essential points of the commercial agreement, identifying the owner, the charterer, the ship, the voyage, the cargo, the freight and other points that are very specific to the fixture.

Then follows a section of the main body of the agreement. It is a standard form which can be amended as required by the parties during negotiation. In order to facilitate this, the text is spaced out and each line is numbered to make modification easy and possible by remote means. For example, a modification might be: 'In Part II, line 21, replace "Manager" with "Managers".'

Bill of lading

When a vessel transports a cargo, the shipper will issue a 'bill of lading'. In effect, this is a receipt issued by the shipper to acknowledge that it has received the cargo in good order and will transport it to the destination given and then make it available to the party named on the bill of lading. The document, of which there will often be a number of 'original' copies, is very important, as it is evidence of the contract to carry the goods and may contain further important contractual information. It is evidence of the ownership of the cargo and of the apparent quantity and condition of the cargo when received. This topic is too complex to consider in any great detail in a book such as this but, in addition to issues of ownership, applicable rules and agreed limitation of the shipper's liabilities, it is a negotiable document and can be used as security for loans.

Hague Rules

This was the first international convention to establish rules for the carriage of goods by sea, including the definitions and limitations of the contract of carriage. It was signed in 1924 and ratified by more than 100 countries. It was intended to provide a uniform level of protection for shippers and carriers and prevent one or other party from seeking to shift all liability to the other party.

The Rules state that the carrier's main duties are to 'properly and carefully load, handle, stow, carry, keep, care for, and discharge the goods carried' and to 'exercise due diligence to ... make the ship seaworthy' and to '... properly man, equip and supply the ship'. It is implicit that the carrier must not deviate from the agreed route nor from the usual route; but Article IV (4) provides that 'any deviation in saving or attempting to save life or property at sea or any reasonable deviation shall not be deemed to be an infringement or breach of these Rules'.

Hague-Visby Rules

The Hague Rules were amended in 1968 and became known as the Hague-Visby Rules, which were ratified by some 25 states. They were further amended in 1979. Most of the amendments were to remove anomalies and to help with interpretations of the value of the cargo.

Hamburg Rules

This convention was signed in 1978 and has been ratified by 34 states. It extends the carrier's liabilities to cover the period from when the carrier receives the cargo to when it releases it (the Hague Rules only covered the time from loading on the ship to discharge from the ship). It also removed the need for a bill of lading in order to force compliance with the rules.

100

The Hamburg Rules were an attempt to balance the risk between carrier and shipper, but the shippers felt that they had been given a raw deal. The Hamburg Rules, however, were seen by the carriers as shifting more of the risk onto the carrier. It may be that the squeals of protest mean that, by and large, both sets of rules are equitable.

Rotterdam Rules

This convention was signed in 2009. To date, it has 20 signatories but has not yet entered into force. It brings the rules for the carriage of goods into the 21st century by incorporating the concept of intermodal transport and extending a carrier's liabilities from the point at which it takes possession of the cargo until the point of delivery, even if this involves transportation by road or rail as well as by ship. It is intended to facilitate e-commerce and the use of electronic documentation.

Worldscale

Before World War II, tanker charters were not dissimilar to dry bulk charters, and in almost every case the actual cargo and the ports were known in advance, so the disponent owner could calculate its costs before making an offer to the charterer. During this war, the British government took over the movement of oil cargo for the war effort, the vessels being 'time chartered' by the government. As the oil companies still needed to carry their own cargoes, they were allowed to use available vessels as long as they compensated the government financially. This was done in accordance with a standard scale of rates that gave a charge from every reasonable combination of port A and port B.

This continued until 1948 and, by then, the tanker business had become accustomed to the convenience of this arrangement, as it did not require precision over port A and port B before the voyage. The chartering market continued to use the Ministry of Transport (MOT) (British government) or United States Maritime Commission (USMC) (US government) rate scales, but these were replaced by trade association scales in the 1950s, with the most notable being International Tanker Nominal Freight Scale Association (Intascale) and American Tanker Rate Schedule (ATRS) scales. These were then replaced in 1969 by Worldscale. This rate scale was calculated for all port combinations using a standard size of ship, agreed voyage distances and standard operating costs. It was updated every six months up to 1988, when it became an annual exercise to reflect realistic fuel and port costs with the new flat rate starting on 1 January each year. The voyage charter would be negotiated as a percentage of the Worldscale flat rate in US$ per tonne for the actual voyage performed. The percentage of the flat rate would reflect the actual ship size and the supply and demand in the market. The standard ship was changed in 1985 and is currently based on a ship of 75,000 DWT with a hire charge of $12,000 per day.

International Commerce Terms (INCOTERMS)

INCOTERMS allocate the duties and liabilities of buyers and sellers of goods where international transport is involved, and the terms are often incorporated in bills of lading. The terms are drawn up by the International Chamber of Commerce (ICC) and the most recent terms are dated 2010. There is a summary of the terms in Appendix 3.

Contract of Affreightment (COA)

Some cargo interests, having very regular requirements, may enter into a contract that covers an agreed number of voyages over a particular time with the charter rate (or the basis for that rate) negotiated at the start of the contract. Thereafter, the cargo interest only has to give the agreed notice (typically, a number of weeks) of the load port and date, as the charter rate has already been pre-agreed. This type of Contract of Affreightment (COA) is common when the total number of voyages does not represent full employment for just one ship but will allow the disponent owner the flexibility to use different ships under its control for each voyage. It is rather like having a contract with a taxi company.

Time chartering

For charterers who are very active in particular trades, if they have enough cargo freight requirement to fully employ one ship then they may contract the whole ship for a period of time (a time charter). They take over the responsibility for voyage orders, where to go, what to load and discharge, etc. They are also responsible for all fuel costs and all port charges. They become the disponent owners of the vessel but the crew, maintenance, insurance and other owner's matters remain the responsibility of the vessel owner.

A time charterer will usually have the freedom to commit the vessel for voyage charters to carry cargo other than its own. A time charter can cover various periods, from three months up to, say, five years. The charter agreement may include options to extend the period of hire at a rate set at the time of negotiating the original charter agreement. The vessel will be delivered to the charterer at an agreed location (usually with a certain quantity of fuel onboard). Towards completion of the agreed period, the time charterer will advise the head owner where the ship is to be redelivered to the owner at the end of the agreed period (usually with a similar amount of fuel onboard). This process is like hiring a car with a driver for a set period.

The example of the time charter included in Appendix 3 shows the first four pages of a 10-page document. It would usually have numbered lines (just like the example of the voyage charter party) to facilitate amendments and corrections. The first four pages cover most of the specifically agreed points of negotiation.

Trip time chartering

The dry bulk trade has no equivalent of Worldscale. It has to deal with situations where the cargo interest does not know in advance at which port it will load (only the general area or country) or the port where it will discharge. This has led to the trip time charter, where the vessel is engaged on a time charter basis for an indeterminate period for one cargo trip only. The charterer has to redeliver the ship back to the owner in a specific area and otherwise accepts all the responsibilities of a time charterer.

Bareboat chartering

A bareback charter is sometimes called a charter by demise, especially when the period is very long and where full ownership may be transferred permanently to the charterer at the conclusion of the charter period. The charterer takes over all the responsibilities of the owner for a period of time, including manning, maintenance, insurance and all the operations and employment of the vessel. A bareboat charter will usually be for five or seven years but can be longer. The vessel will frequently enter this kind of charter on delivery from a shipyard and it is commonly employed by oil companies and some container ship companies. The charterer must return the vessel at the end of the agreed period in good order, fully maintained but with an understanding that there will be fair wear and tear (i.e. the vessel will not be returned 'as new').

Shipbroking

Shipbrokers are intermediaries who market 'open' ships to cargo interests and circulate cargo voyages to shipowners. They were the go-betweens in the old style exchanges where ships were matched with cargoes, being investors and market participants themselves.

In smaller ports, ship agents acted as shipbrokers but, by the 19th century, brokers started to set up offices specialising in the finding and fixing of ships and cargo. Most of the biggest broking firms are in London, New York and Singapore, although there are many in Oslo, Hamburg and other places who would challenge this comment.

A shipbroker is central to the negotiation of the charter party and will follow the deal from initial enquiry to the final settlement of all payments. There are various specialisations – tankers, dry cargo, container ships, offshore, gas tankers and, especially, sale and purchase. A shipbroker typically earns a commission of 1.25% of the total freight payment but is expected to provide support to both principals throughout the contract. It will usually have an operations department dealing with queries and communications after the deal has been fixed, and a demurrage or claims department to handle outstanding issues after the completion of the voyage.

A good shipbroker is a provider of shipping and financial research, a negotiator and, in case of disputes, a good mediator. It used to be the case there would be two brokers participating, one acting for the disponent owner and another for the charterer, each earning 1.25% of the freight as a broker's commission. Today, it is far more common that only one broker is involved in the deal.

The charter negotiations will be very detailed and cover a number of commercially significant issues. Once the deal is concluded, the broker will send an electronic summary of all of the agreed terms of the charter to the principals. This message is called a 'recap' and at this point the vessel is said to be 'fixed'. It will be followed by a formal complete document, the charter party, which will be signed by both principals. Sometimes an agreement will be reached on all major points but with some specific points awaiting final clarification. Under these conditions, a vessel is said to be 'fixed on subjects' and the 'subjects' will be clearly defined in the recap, e.g. 'subject terminal approval of vessel' or 'subject final management approval'. If these are not forthcoming, then the vessel will 'fail' and the charter will not go ahead.

Ship vetting

Most charterers will want to satisfy themselves that a vessel which they will use to carry their cargo or that they will time charter is in 'good order' and will meet their own minimum standards. This has become a more stringent requirement in the shipping industry and extends beyond the physical condition of the ship to encompass crew experience and the management and financial condition of the owning company.

Tanker vetting

By 1985, most oil majors had their own inspection teams, visiting and inspecting prospective vessels and checking documentation, onboard procedures, physical condition and, in the case of time charters, auditing the vessel's management. This reached a stage where a vessel arriving at a large oil terminal might be visited by four or more inspectors from different oil companies. In order to rationalise this process, the Oil Companies International Marine Forum (OCIMF) established a vetting system and database called the Ship Inspection Report programme (SIRE). This system uses contracted inspectors working to an agreed standard and submitting reports which are then shared by all members of SIRE. An operator should ensure that a vessel has a current SIRE inspection report available if it wants to get the ship accepted. In 2004, the SIRE system was expanded to include barges and small vessels.

Dry bulk vetting

This has been growing since the late 1990s. There are a number of commercial companies performing this task, and the best known is Rightship. It does not always inspect ships but compiles its rating from published data. The following extract is taken from the Rightship website.

The risk rating is determined by a computer-based algorithm. It calculates risk based on data collected under about 50 risk factors, including the following as well as other factors:

- *Flag Risk (determined by statistical assessment of PSC inspection, casualty and Incident performance associated with the particular flag)*

- *Class Risk (determined by statistical assessment of PSC inspection, casualty and Incident performance associated with the particular class society)*

- *Number of Changes of flag, class, owner or manager*

- *The vessel's casualty history*

- *The vessel's berth reports*

- *The vessel's terminal reports*

- *The vessel's PSC performance (including particular attention to multiple deficiencies and/or detentions over a period of time)*

- *The vessel's age.*

These and other risk factors go towards a 'score', which is then combined with other factors (such as Port State Control performance) to determine the overall star rating. Ships rated as highest risk score less than 72 through the system, while ships rated as lowest risk can score anywhere over 120. Ships scoring 88 and over are likely to be rated as a satisfactory risk without further review.

(Reproduced with kind permission of Rightship.)

Chapter 11 - Major cost elements

As can be seen from the preceding sections, the allocation of costs will depend on the nature of the chartering of the vessel. This section will address each cost on the basis of a ship operated by the head owner and engaged in direct trade for that owner.

To put this into context, the data below covers only the owner's operating costs, and it excludes the financial charges and the variable costs of the voyage (bunkers, port costs, canal dues, etc.). This is a breakdown from just one ship management company operating dry bulk and container ships between 1,500 DWT and 10,000 DWT.

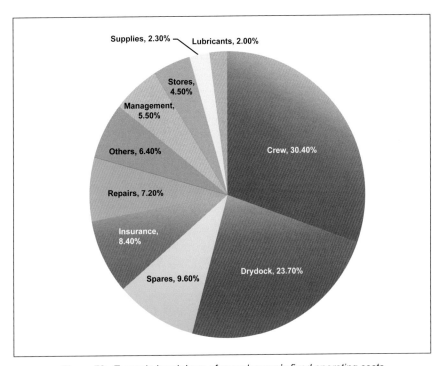

Figure 72. Example breakdown of vessel owner's fixed operating costs

Bulkers	
Handy	$5,500
Handymax	$6,250
Panamax	$6,750
Capesize	$7,750

Tankers	
GP	$8,500
MR	$8,400
LR1	$8,700
LR2	$9,900
VLCC	$11,000

Container	
Feeder	$4,600
Feedermax	$5,400
Panamax	$7,850

Operating costs per day for different ship types (2013 estimates) – excluding bunkers, port costs and canal dues. This data is taken from a survey of a number of ship operating companies.

Manning

Most vessel staff and crew in merchant shipping are employed directly by the owner as contractors (probably via a manning agency). The owner is responsible for wages, social costs, healthcare and food whilst the crew are onboard the ship. Many good owners will also pay for training, travel to and from the vessel, and for agreed periods of leave. The cost per crew member depends on experience, seniority onboard and certificates held. As the crew can be drawn from a variety of countries, levels of pay can vary enormously and cannot be easily compared. However, as an illustration, a ship's Master can earn up to 10 times the pay of a junior rating.

Maintenance

Vessel maintenance is a continuing charge over the life of the ship. Routine onboard maintenance performed by the crew is comparatively cheap (stripping out the cost of spare parts and consumables such as paint). However, some equipment will need specialist maintenance by technicians from a manufacturer or a company skilled and experienced in dealing with specific equipment.

Vessels are required by their classification society to undergo inspection and surveys at regular intervals, some of which will need to be carried out with the vessel out of service but afloat whilst others will require the vessel to enter dry dock. The usual interval for inspections in dock is two years, with classification societies allowing a 'grace period' of six months. If the vessel carries out very specific and detailed inspections afloat they may be able to defer dry dock inspection for a further period of two years (with another six-month grace period). Such a procedure will allow the dry dock periods to coincide with the 'special survey' which must take place every five years.

As a consequence of the above, most tankers and bulk carriers will only enter dry dock once every five years. The requirements for some other types of vessel are much stricter and some vessels will dock every year. In shipping company accounts, the maintenance costs for each year will include a fifth of the estimated cost of the next dry dock.

Stores and spares

All the material (excluding fuel) consumed onboard by the crew in the course of their duties is regarded as stores. This covers food, replacement linen, paint, tools, charts – everything. It is one of the categories included in the deadweight of the ship. Engine room stores will include chemicals, steel, brass and copper stock materials for fabricating some parts onboard, as well as a huge selection of nuts, bolts, screws, jointing materials and other consumables needed for routine maintenance. Spare parts for all the equipment, some of which are extraordinarily expensive, are a separate cost item and are not included in the deadweight.

A classification society will insist on certain spares being carried onboard but the owner will decide on what to carry over and above that minimum. Fifty years ago, almost every ship carried a spare propeller and spare main shafting even though these could only be changed at a shipyard, but as air transport has reduced transit times, fewer large items are carried.

Insurance

Hull and machinery insurance is paid for by an annual premium to the insurers. As already stated, this is not a requirement but very few owners do not carry insurance. There will also be a premium for special insurance to cover special provisions for oil pollution (certificates of financial responsibility for vessels entering the United States, for example). The owner will also have its ship entered into a P&I club and this will require payment of the annual 'call', and possibly an additional call if the club has had a 'bad' year.

Bunkering

Ships' fuel is called bunkers and in current markets they can represent up to 80 % of the variable costs of a voyage. Fuel is priced in US$ per tonne and must be paid for usually within 21 or 30 days of the delivery to the vessel. The fuel is paid for by the disponent owner, so this could be the head owner, a bareboat charterer or a time charterer. Most ships burn a residual fuel oil that has to be treated and heated onboard before it can be used; it is one of the cheapest forms of fuel available. Small ships will burn marine gasoil (MGO) that is very similar to the diesel fuel used in road transport. Larger ships may use MGO for generating electricity onboard.

If a ship is sailing in an area where the level of sulphur (SOx) is controlled (an emission control area (ECA)), then the restriction will require the vessel to use only fuel with a very low sulphur level. This means that it will have to use MGO for all purposes whilst sailing in this area. It can continue to use high sulphur residual fuel if the vessel is equipped with exhaust gas treatment plant (scrubbers) but, at the time of writing, less than 100 ships are so equipped. This figure will quickly increase as we progress towards 2020 when the sulphur restrictions will start to apply to much wider areas. By 2025 there will be a worldwide limit of 0.5% sulphur in bunker fuel. The sulphur restrictions will have a major impact on the cost of fuel. This topic is dealt with in more detail in the sections on *MARPOL* and *Atmospheric Pollution*.

Port charges

When a vessel enters a port there are a number of discrete payments to be made. These are generally combined and referred to as port charges, or port costs. The following list is not exhaustive.

Port dues
Pilotage
Towage
Wharfage
Environmental levy
Waste levy
Line handling
Launch services
Agency fee
Light dues
Cargo dues
Anchorage dues
Fire watch charges

Many ports now charge a consolidated fee to simplify the above payments but those shaded in blue will not be included in the consolidated dues.

Port dues and charges levied by the port operator used to be based on the net tonnage of a vessel but it is becoming more common to see them charged based on gross tonnage (GT).

Port dues will usually be settled by the vessel agent. When the owner advises the agent of its intention to call at a port and appoints that agent to act on its behalf, the agent will submit a pro forma disbursement account to the owner estimating the total cost of the port call. The agent will usually expect the owner to transfer the required funds so that the payments can be made to the port authority, port operator, towage company, etc. in a timely manner.

Chapter 12 - Ship propulsion

With the exception of the few sailing vessels in merchant service, all ships need engines for their propulsion. The principal propulsion for almost all ships is by propeller. The ship will also need generators for electrical power and dozens of pumps, heaters, coolers and other pieces of mechanical equipment to keep the ship running, to take care of the crew and passengers, and to look after the cargo.

Engines

Almost all merchant ships use diesel engines for propulsion and to generate electricity. These engines range from small high-speed engines through to medium-speed engines, which can weigh as much as 50 tonnes and produce 30,000 horsepower, up to slow-speed engines. To date, the largest slow-speed engines are installed on the *Emma Maersk*, weighing 2,300 tonnes and producing 120,000 horsepower whilst turning at no more than 95 revolutions per minute (rpm). Medium-speed and slow-speed engines use residual fuel oil that is black, thick and smelly. It requires treatment and heating onboard before use but costs much less than gasoil. High-speed engines use gasoil which is very similar to automotive fuel for diesel cars and trucks.

A few ships still use steam propulsion. Steam is generated by boiling water in large boilers and it is used to power turbines that drive the propeller via a big gearbox. This type of propulsion is now limited to nuclear propulsion (warships and icebreakers) and to a large number of LNG tankers.

Some vessels also use gas turbine propulsion, but this is limited to some warships, fast ferries and some cruise liners.

Figure 73. MAN B & W G60 ME-C 6 cylinder engine

Photograph courtesy of MAN Diesel & Turbo (www.mandieselturbo.com)

The largest MAN B & W slow speed engines are over 13 m high, and 27 m long and have 14 cylinders.

Propellers

The propeller is one of the largest components on a ship. It is made of a special bronze alloy, and on very big tankers the propellers can weigh up to 130 tonnes and have a diameter of over 10 m. Most ships have one propeller although some have two (twin screw ships). The propeller is part of a screw with three, four or five threads, which gives three, four or five blades to the propeller.

Figure 74. A five-bladed propeller

Photograph courtesy of Nigel Draffin

Most ships have fixed pitch propellers. If the ship needs to go backwards (astern) then the direction of rotation has to be changed. Some ships have propellers which permit the angle of the blades to be adjusted whilst they are turning, and this allows the ship to go astern without changing the direction of rotation. This type of propeller is called a controllable pitch propeller.

Manoeuvring

When moving inside a port or transiting restricted waters, a ship will need to vary its speed and direction. This is done by adjusting the speed of the propeller (usually by varying the speed of the main engine) and changing the direction of the propeller thrust from ahead to astern (see the note above). The ship will turn and change course by use of its rudder, which is powered by steering gear mounted inside the hull above the rudder (usually operated by hydraulic power) or, on some ships, by changing the thrust axis of special propulsion pods hanging under the hull (see *Azimuthing thrusters*). Many modern vessels also have transverse thrusters (as described earlier, under the section on *Mooring*).

Figure 75. Rudder and controllable pitch propeller

Photograph courtesy of Nigel Draffin

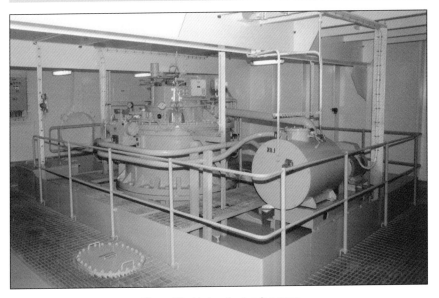

Figure 76. Hydraulic steering gear

Photograph courtesy of Nigel Draffin

Figure 77. Azimuthing thrusters before installation in a ship

Photograph courtesy of Kovako-1 (CCO 1.0)

The ideal combination is a very large diameter propeller turning relatively slowly. In their ability to meet this ideal, the tanker or bulk carrier come closest because they have the available space below the water at the stern and use very long stroke engines turning as slow as 60 rpm at full power. A container ship, because of the requirements of the cargo space, does not have as much space and its engines will therefore run at a higher rotational speed.

High-speed vessels, such as fast ferries, pose a problem for propellers as the high flow rate over the blades causes a phenomenon called cavitation that damages the propeller surface. To avoid this, these vessels use devices called water jets that are submerged water pumps producing a high-speed jet of water out of the rear. The water jet is equipped with baffles to reverse the direction of thrust for astern operation.

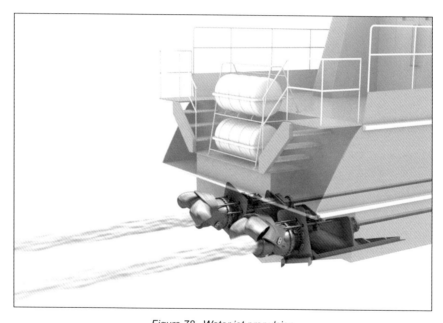

Figure 78. Water jet propulsion

Image courtesy of Rolls-Royce plc (www.rolls-royce.com)

Speed

Ship speed is a difficult issue. The faster you go the more voyages you can perform each year and the more revenue you will generate, but the amount of fuel consumed increases according to a cube law and rises very much more than the vessel speed. Speed is therefore a compromise between income and costs. In order to get the most efficient hull shape, the naval architect needs to know the desired speed. The optimum hull shape for your ship size and draught will only be optimum at one speed. Designers try to arrange reasonable to good fuel efficiency over a limited range of draught and speed, with the optimum at the 'design' speed and 'design' draught. Most ocean-going ships are designed for speeds of between 14-16 knots (nautical miles per hour), and they will be capable of operating for long periods at speeds of 60% of design speed without taking any special precautions and up to 5% above design speed for shorter periods.

Tankers and bulkers are usually designed for speeds of 14 knots, reefer ships for up to 25 knots, and the most modern container ships for about 22 knots.

High-speed ferries, such as those operating in the Mediterranean, can operate at well over 40 knots.

The table below gives some examples of vessel design speeds.

Ship type	Size	Design speed in knots	Fuel consumption per day (mt)
Bulk carrier	5,000 DWT	10	7
Bulk carrier	25,000 DWT	13	13.5
Bulk carrier	65,000 DWT	14.5	28
Bulk carrier	175,000 DWT	14	64
Container ship	1,000 TEU	15.5	12
Container ship	2,300 TEU	18	42
Container ship	8,800 TEU	23	155
Container ship	18,000 TEU	21	250
Reefer	10,000 TEU	22	60
Tanker	8,000 DWT	13.5	16
Tanker	80,000 DWT	15.5	38
Tanker	150,000 DWT	15.5	58
Tanker	300,000 DWT	15	90

Hull shape – the shape of the hull has a huge effect on the power required to move the vessel at normal speeds. The naval architect looks for a couple of guidelines and these help him to calculate the power needed to achieve the speed the owner wants.

1. The coefficient of the fineness of the water plane area (the area of the horizontal cross-section of the hull at the waterline) that compares the actual area of the water plane with the theoretical area of a rectangle of the same length and breadth.

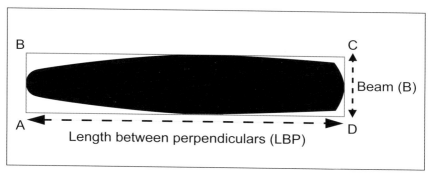

Figure 79. Water plane

2. The block coefficient of the fineness, which compares the actual volume under water with the theoretical volume of a shape the same length, breadth and depth.

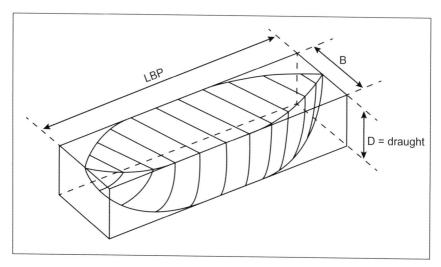

Figure 80. Block coefficient

Efficiency

Once the ship is built, as long as the shipping market stays constant then all is well, but in practice the market is constantly changing and the owner will look for ways to improve the efficiency of its vessels.

Same power less fuel

This involves finding ways to improve the energy efficiency of the machinery. It can be achieved by changing the operational parameters of the engine, possibly by changing some of the components (different designs of fuel injectors, changes to the turbocharging system) or by changing the temperatures and pressures in the plant. This is especially true where the ship has a waste heat system to extract heat from the exhaust gas.

Less speed less fuel

This involves running the ship at a lower speed and benefiting from the fact that the fuel consumption decreases much faster than the loss of speed. This is often called 'slow steaming' and has been a useful tool for ship operators for many decades. The trick is to balance the decreased annual earnings (fewer voyages and less freight income) against reduced fuel costs. It was much easier to manage with big steamships as they could operate continuously at very low speeds (less than 6 knots or 10% power) whilst diesel engine vessels were not able to run much below 70% power for extended periods. Recent developments in diesel engine design have given diesel ships much more flexibility and, subject to changes in operational routines, they can now run for extended periods at 30% power or less.

Same speed less power

This can be achieved by improving the hydrodynamic performance of the hull and the propeller by, for example, cleaning the ship's hull to remove accumulated marine growth and polishing the surface of the propeller blades to improve the propeller's performance. It can also be improved when the ship is sailing in ballast by adjusting the ballast draught and by adjusting the ballast trim (the difference between the draught at the bow and the draught at the stern).

Greenhouse gases (GHG)

Regulatory authorities have expressed major concerns over the levels of carbon dioxide (CO_2) and other pollutants emitted from ship exhaust. Most authorities believe that global warming is a phenomenon linked to the actions of these pollutants and one of the obvious remedies is to reduce the amount of pollutants emitted. The amount of CO_2 emitted is directly linked to the amount of fuel consumed, so the IMO, through the MARPOL convention, has instituted some compulsory and some voluntary measures to drive this.

Energy Efficiency Design Index (EEDI)

This allows owners and designers to establish the EEDI for their new ships from calculated data. By comparing the EEDI of a new ship design against the norm for its peers, the efficiency of the design can be compared and the industry can be tasked with reducing the EEDI for new designs over a period of time.

Ship Energy Efficiency Management Plan (SEEMP)

Owners must show that they are actively measuring their energy efficiency and using the SEEMP to improve the efficiency over time. The plan applies to existing ships as well as new ships.

The areas that would be included in the SEEMP are: fuel efficient operations; optimised ship handling; hull and propeller optimisation; machinery optimisation; cargo handling optimisation and energy conservation. For each of these headings, the plan must detail the intended action, the method of implementation and the methods of monitoring and recording.

Energy Efficiency Operational Index (EEOI)

This is a measure of the CO_2 generated per 'capacity mile', where the capacity element can be tonnes of cargo, number of containers, number of passengers or any relevant measure of the cargo carried. The EEOI will be different on each leg of a voyage and may be calculated for each leg or taken as a rolling average. It is a tool to monitor the energy efficiency in a consistent way over time for each ship. Its use is voluntary.

Chapter 13 - Sale and purchase

Vessel owners purchase ships as either new builds from a shipyard or second-hand from another owner. The cost of the vessel will depend on its complexity, age, condition and, most importantly, the current shipping market conditions. Most owners will require a source of finance for their purchases and this will usually be in the form of a mortgage from a bank, which might be for as much as 90% of the cost.

If the shipping market deteriorates after the vessel has been purchased, the market value of the ship may be lower than the amount that the owner has borrowed. Experienced owners will devote a lot of time and effort to watching the market and they will try to buy at a time when vessel values are at their lowest. They will also be prepared to sell the vessel when they believe the market is approaching its highest point. There is an opportunity to make much more money buying and selling the ship than there is from just trading it to carry cargo. There is also a big risk for any bank lending money to an owner in a mortgage if the owner is unable to make the payments on his loan as this will usually be at a time when the market is bad, vessel values are low and the hull value of the ship may then be much lower than the value of the loan. The sale and purchase deals are handled by a specialist shipbroker who will be involved in putting the deal together and negotiating with the buyer, the seller and the participating banks.

New ships

New ships are built in shipyards which either specialise in particular ship types or are capable of building a large range of ship types and sizes. A new ship takes between six months and one year to build but may be ordered up to three years before the expected completion date. The majority of merchant shipbuilding is concentrated in the Far East and there are many yards in South Korea, Japan and China. The shipyards in Northern Europe and in the United States have high labour costs so they tend to specialise in complex, high value ships or small ships for local trade where the cost of the long delivery voyage to Europe from the Far East makes the European yard price more attractive.

Ships used to be built on land and then 'slipped' into the water after the hull was completed. This method has largely been superseded by building the ship in a graving dock and flooding the dock when the hull is completed.

Some of the shipyards' graving docks are big enough to build two or three ships at a time. The owner will have a small team of superintendents on site and there will also be surveyors from the classification society and from the flag State to ensure that the vessel complies with all of the applicable rules and regulations.

Once the construction is completed, the ship will be named, commissioned and will undergo sea trials to ensure all is working well before it is handed over to the owner. As soon as the order is placed, the vessel will be given a unique number, the IMO number (which is often called the Lloyd's number). It will also have a yard hull number to identify the ship until it is named by the owner. The IMO number stays with the ship, irrespective of how many times it is bought and sold or has its name changed, until the vessel is scrapped.

The owner will pay for the ship in stages – an initial deposit, further payments at intervals during the construction, and final payment when the owner accepts the ship at the end of the commissioning and trials. Although the ship may cost many hundreds of millions of dollars, the shipyard will only guarantee the ship and its equipment for a period of one year!

Figure 81. 300-tonne gantry crane with double trolley for ship building

Photograph courtesy of Encore Cranes (www.encorecranes.com)

Scrapping

At the end of the useful economic life of a vessel it will be sold to a scrap yard for recycling. The scrap yard will remove any machinery that has any life left in it for sale to the second-hand spares market, and it will cut the steel structure up for melting down as steel scrap, Anything which can be sold for raw materials or use will be carefully recovered (steel, copper wire, aluminium, etc.) but the scrap yard will have to deal with any hazardous waste or potential pollutants in a method required by the country in which it operates.

Small ships will be dismantled alongside a quay but most merchant ships are literally run up onto a beach and dismantled there. The biggest scrap yards are in, or near, the Indian sub-continent, where the cost of semi-skilled labour is cheap. The owner will be paid a price per lightship tonne.

The IMO has adopted a convention on ship recycling (the Hong Kong Convention) but it has not yet been ratified. Once it enters in to force, it will change the face of ship recycling in terms of the welfare and safety of the workers in the industry and environmental damage and pollution.

Figure 82. Ship breaking

Photograph courtesy of Maro Kouri 2010 & Shipbreaking Platform (www.shipbreakingplatform.org)

The economic life of a ship is, to a large degree, dependent on the market conditions in its particular sector, the costs of maintenance and insurance (which increase with age) and the impact of keeping the vessel in compliance with new legislation. Some tankers built in the 1970s were sent to scrap after only eight years' service, whilst some passenger vessels are still in service after 50 years of service. The following table lists some average life expectancies.

Vessel type	Typical service life in years
VLCC	25
LNG carrier	40
Dry bulk	30
Passenger	35
Offshore support vessel	40
VL container	25
Feeder container	30
General cargo	40
Reefer	35

The cost of a special dry dock survey (every five years) is often the trigger for a decision to scrap.

Chapter 14 - Finance

Ship owning requires strong finances and even stronger nerves. The shipping market is cyclical and an owner needs to be able to hold back some of the returns in good times to support activity when times are hard. The cost of a modest second-hand ship can be many tens of millions of dollars and the vessel may well need to generate $10,000 to $15,000 per day in income to cover the costs. Putting a ship though its five-yearly special survey will cost millions of dollars.

Ownership structures

The rules on ownership vary from one legal system to another. By 1845, British-flagged ships were either owned by a single individual or by a number of individuals, with the ownership being divided into 64 individual shares. The French system used 24 equal shares. This was to limit the number of names on the registration documents.

As stated earlier, the owner is responsible to the administration of the country where its ship is registered (the flag State) for every aspect of the ship. In practice, many vessels are owned by single ship companies which are private companies set up for the purpose of owning an individual ship. This is to gain the most favourable tax treatment and to limit the exposure of the investors to some liabilities. These companies are often registered in jurisdictions where the identity of the shareholders is *not* a matter of public record.

It has been the practice for a very long time for significant fleets of vessels all 'owned' by an individual or a family to have the vessels owned and registered by single ship companies, although the reality is that, other than the legal ownership, the ships are operated as a single fleet.

In recent years, some investment and ownership structures have emerged to allow smaller investors to participate in ship ownership and to enjoy tax benefits on the returns. Examples of this are the German KG funds, Norwegian KS funds and Netherlands CV funds; all of these take advantage of the special tonnage tax regimes in those countries.

Mortgages

Ships, just like houses, can be used as security for a loan and the most common vehicle for this is a mortgage. Most legal systems provide specific statutory forms of ship mortgage. In the United Kingdom, the *Merchant Shipping Act* provides the following: 'A registered ship, or a share in any such ship, may be made a security for the repayment of a loan or the discharge of any other obligation; and on production of the instrument creating any such security (referred to in this Act as a mortgage), the registrar of the ship's port of registry shall record it in the register.'

The existence of a registered mortgage gives the lender some specific rights to recover its loan by repossessing the ship for sale and it also accords a priority claim on the funds generated after certain specific debts are paid, such as port expenses, crew wages, and claims which are called maritime liens.

Public or private

Many large shipping companies are publicly-quoted companies. This gives them recourse to raising funds on the stock exchange where they are each registered. However, with public ownership comes a parcel of requirements and duties with regards to accounting, reporting facts to shareholders and other legal duties. If an owner wants to operate as a private entity then it can avoid much of this bureaucracy and avoid the difficulties involved in quarterly financial reporting and the need to retain shareholder confidence. However, this owner would not have the ability to raise capital by issuing shares to public investors.

Chapter 15 - Pollution

From the earliest days of ocean transport, seafarers have become used to discarding 'waste' by throwing it over the side. By the 15th century, the residents of ports had started to protest and to regulate the worst excesses, but it was not until the 1960s that the world took maritime pollution seriously. A number of major oil spills from the new supertankers and the quantification of the amount of oil that was discharged at sea during routine tank cleaning onboard led to the establishment of compensation funds to pay for damage caused by oil pollution. In the 1970s, the IMO produced the Convention on Maritime Pollution (MARPOL). It is the annexes to this convention that deal with almost all types of pollution from ships.

Sea

MARPOL regulates and controls the discharge of oil into the sea from any source onboard ship. It regulates the disposal of sludge and oil waste, the disposal of garbage and of human waste. A recent development has been the realisation that because vessels may take on ballast water in one geographical location and then discharge it in a different location they may inadvertently transport living organisms from one eco system to another in which they are not a native species. There is now a Ballast Water Management convention which, when ratified, will require all vessels to treat or sterilise their ballast water either on passage or at the loading port when the ballast is discharged. The convention will need to be ratified by at least 30 states and 35% of global tonnage. At the time of writing, the number of states ratifying is now 36 but the global tonnage is only at 29%, so it still needs one or two more signatories.

Atmosphere

MARPOL also covers the pollution of the atmosphere by engine exhaust. It limits the sulphur content of the fuel (sulphur oxides (SOx) in the exhaust gas) and the nitrous oxides (NOx) in the exhaust gas, the vapours from oil cargo (volatile organic compounds (VOC), and the use of certain refrigerant gases. It may soon be amended to cover soot (particulate matter (PM), and deposits of certain related pollutants, such as black carbon in Arctic waters.

The convention has rules covering all the oceans and different rules apply to particular areas where the risks are higher. In the case of SOx and NOx, there are areas called emission control areas (ECAs) which have much tighter restrictions. At this time, ECAs cover the Baltic Sea, the English Channel, the North Sea, and most of the coast of North America – other ECAs are planned.

The European Union (EU) and the State of California have additional regulations on vessel exhaust which are more restrictive than MARPOL.

Vessels may apply 'abatement technology' to reduce SOx in the exhaust subject to flag State approval and compliance with the rules detailed in MARPOL Annex VI. The current sulphur limits are as follows:

Global limit 3.5% from 1 January 2012 (in effect now)

Global limit reduced to 0.50% from 1 January 2020 (subject to availability review in 2018 which could defer reduction until 2025)

ECA limit 1.00% from July 2010 (in effect now)

ECA limit further reduced to 0.10% from 1 January 2015.

This applies to all liquid fuel used.

The EU requires that all ships at berth alongside or securely anchored within an EU port must only burn fuel with a maximum of 0.1% sulphur. The EU has also stated its intention to introduce a 0.5% cap in EU waters from 2020.

Chapter 16 - Safety

Responsibilities

The Master of every ship is responsible for the safety of the crew, the passengers, the ship, and the cargo, as well as the safety of the navigation of the ship. Many of these responsibilities are devolved to other officers onboard and the Master has a right to expect them to be aware of all of those responsibilities where this is supported by licences and certificates of competency awarded by their flag State.

The principal risks onboard are collision, fire and explosion but there are many others linked to the operation and maintenance of the vessel. Everyday tasks involve the lifting and moving of heavy components, handling wires and ropes under tension and the need for crew to work aloft with the attendant risks of falling. Each man in the crew is responsible for his own safety but the officers must ensure that all appropriate precautions are taken and that full use is made of all personal protective clothing and equipment (which must be provided by the ship).

Distress

Each vessel has equipment to protect and save life should the vessel be in extreme peril. Fire fighting equipment and systems, lifeboats and life rafts are mandatory and their use must be practised by all the crew. The crew will also have to assist any passengers to ensure their safety. If a vessel has a situation onboard which the Master deems to be sufficiently serious to require help from outside the ship then he has the ability to call for help using the Global Maritime Distress and Safety System (GMDSS) or by any other means. Any other ship in the vicinity receiving that call for assistance is duty bound, if practical (depending on time and distance), to proceed to the distressed ship to render assistance. In practice, there are a number of maritime distress coordinating stations around the world and they will identify the nearest ships to the casualty and request them to assist. This is written into the SOLAS convention, into UNCLOS and into the Search and Rescue convention (SAR).

Piracy

Piracy is as old as waterborne transport. By the early 1900s, through the actions of powerful navies, it had been reduced to a minority occupation. Whilst never completely going away, it was confined to limited attacks in some under-developed coastal states – until the end of the 20th century. Over the last 10 years, there has been a tremendous growth in piracy off the coast of some states, especially Somalia, in the Strait of Malacca and the area between Côte d'Ivoire and Nigeria. Somali pirates can seek to detain a vessel and her crew until paid a ransom (sometimes totalling many millions of dollars). Off Malacca, the objective is usually theft of money and crew possessions, whilst off West Africa it often involves theft of the cargo (especially petroleum products).

Pirates target slow-moving vessels and can threaten, and use, extreme violence. Concerted action by naval vessels has suppressed the activity to some degree, as has the maintenance of security procedures and the carriage of security staff on merchant vessels when in danger areas. There is still a concern over the use of armed guards as well as the insurance costs associated with kidnap and ransom cover.

Present day pirates use small open boats to launch their attacks and, initially, this served to limit their operating range. However, they now increasingly use captured vessels as 'mother' ships, and this allows them to operate much further from home. It also increases the area that needs to be patrolled by naval vessels and thereby reduces the chances of interception. Information on piracy is coordinated and collected by the International Maritime Bureau Piracy Reporting Centre (IMB PRC).

International Bargaining Forum (IBF)

In some areas, because of the physical risks to a vessel's personnel due to war situations or risk of piracy, hijack and kidnap, the crew are paid double wages and also receive increased benefits to compensate for injury or death. A crew also has the right to refuse to sail in a high risk area. The International Bargaining Forum (IBF) is a negotiating forum for various national shipowners' organisations and the International Transport Workers' Federation (ITF). This forum decides which areas will be treated as high risk.

Salvage

If a ship in distress cannot proceed under her own power, or if the crew has had to abandon the vessel, then it is likely that the owner will engage the services of a salvor. This is a company which will undertake to rescue the ship and bring her safely to port. This operation is called salvage and, historically, the salvor would be engaged under a special contract (Lloyd's Open Form (LOF)) where, if the salvor did not succeed, it would not receive any money (no cure, no pay). If it did succeed, it would be awarded a significant part of the value of the ship and the cargo saved.

Today, because of the need to protect the environment, and the fact that the salvor could devote a lot of time and effort to containing oil spills and ensuring that the vessel did not hazard other ships or property and yet could end up with nothing, this is no longer an acceptable principle. A new clause has been added to LOF, the SCOPIC clause, which ensures that the salvor receives appropriate payment for the work done even if the vessel is not saved.

Another element of salvage is the 'removal of wreck', where the owner can be required to have the wreck of its vessel physically removed if it poses a risk to other ships. This work will be contracted to a salvage company and, in general, is covered by the owner's insurance.

This work can be vital. In 2002, for example, the car carrier *Tricolor* was in collision with the container ship *Kariba* 20 miles from the coast of France. The *Tricolor* sank, resting on her side in 30 metres' depth of water at the junction of the Traffic Separation Scheme channels. The French authorities ordered the wreck to be removed and it was immediately placed under watch by one French police vessel, one British warship and two salvage vessels, and marked with three wreck buoys. Despite this, another vessel collided with the wreck the following night. Two additional patrol ships were added to the protective ring and six more wreck buoys installed. The following night another ship hit the wreck!

Permanent removal commenced just over three months later. After cutting the wreck into nine sections using carbide chain saws, each section, complete with its (ruined) cargo of expensive cars, was lifted by floating crane – 3,000 tonnes at a time – and landed onshore for demolition. The whole operation took 15 months.

Figure 83. Salvage operation to recover the Tricolor

Photograph courtesy of DEME Group (www.deme-group.com)

Another more recent and ambitious project was the removal of the cruise liner *Costa Concordia* from the seashore on the Island of Giglio, off the Italian coast. The project commenced in May 2013.

Figure 84. Costa Concordia *with caissons installed on the port side*

Photograph courtesy of Isjc 99 (CY BY-SA 3.0)

The salvors installed flotation tanks (caissons) on the port side of the *Costa Concordia* (Summer 2013) and then used wires and winches to pull the vessel upright (September 2013). At the time of writing, they are installing caissons on the starboard side in preparation for towing the ship away to a shipyard for demolition (towards the end of 2014).

Chapter 17 - Shipping organisations

Non-governmental organisations (NGOs)

These are organisations that represent special interests or specific industries. The organisations listed below all have consultancy status at the IMO and participate fully in its discussions and in the work of its various working and correspondence groups.

BIMCO – Baltic and International Maritime Council

CLIA – Cruise Lines International Association

IACS – International Association of Classification Societies

IBIA – International Bunker Industry Association

ICS – International Chamber of Shipping

IHMA – International Harbour Masters' Association

INTERCARGO – International Association of Dry Cargo Shipowners

INTERFERRY – International Association of Ferry Owners

INTERTANKO – International Association of Independent Tanker Owners

ISU – International Salvage Union

ITF – International Transport Workers' Federation

ITOPF – International Tanker Owners' Pollution Federation

OCIMF – Oil Companies International Maritime Forum

SIGTTO – Society of Gas Tanker and Terminal Operators

Inter-governmental organisations (IGOs)

These are organisations that provide for cooperation on a variety of matters between groups of national governments. The list below is just a selection; they all have observer status at the IMO.

ACS – Association of Caribbean States

AU – African Union

CARICOM – Caribbean Community

EC – European Commission

IHO – International Hydrographic Organization

INTERPOL – International Criminal Police Organization

IWC – International Whaling Commission

There are also eight separate MoU organisations (see page 74).

Chapter 18 - Legal issues

Disputes

As with all contractual arrangements, there will be disagreements between counter parties over various aspects of their agreement, especially when things are not running smoothly. These disputes can be between the head owner and a time charterer over the performance of the vessel, between the buyer of fuel and the supplier of the fuel, between the disponent owner and the provider of services in the port (chandlers, tug companies, etc.). All of these disputes need to be dealt with in accordance with the provisions of the contract agreed between the counter parties.

Experience shows that most of these disputes can be avoided by careful attention to detail. One of the biggest pitfalls for any party making a claim against their counter party is to make its claim outside the time frame laid down in the contract. This is called a 'time bar'; any claim filed too late will be 'time barred' and will almost always fail.

The pursuit of a claim will require the presentation of documentary evidence to support the claim. In some cases, this will comprise basic documentation, such as log books, time sheets and contemporaneous notes, etc. In other cases, however, there may be considerable differences in the interpretation of facts to determine the cause of the dispute. Unsurprisingly, as these claims can involve very large amounts of money, there is a sizeable industry of maritime lawyers, expert witnesses, surveyors and others who are engaged by both parties to present their respective cases.

Ship arrest

When a party believes that the disponent owner owes it money, it may then have the ability to apply to the courts in a port where the ship is currently located to have the ship arrested in order to force the alleged debtor to pay its debt. The mechanism varies from state to state but its origins began with the party which held the claim being required to show evidence to the court that there was indeed a debt (even if the liabilities had not yet been fully determined). The port would then issue an arrest warrant (originally 'nailed to the mast' on wooden ships), which forbade the ship from sailing out of the port.

Once a warrant has been issued, the port will prevent the vessel from sailing until security has been posted with the court to cover the amount of the dispute. Once this has been done, the ship can then be released and returned to earning money. These days, the security will usually be posted by the P&I club of the owner. The merits of the case will then be decided by formal proceedings, with the claimant knowing in advance that if its claim succeeds then it will be paid from the security that was posted.

Ship arrest is a very complex topic; anyone involved should take professional advice from lawyers familiar with the procedures and requirements of the state where the arrest has been made. Some ports and national laws have a reputation as being very 'good' for ship arrest, whilst others are seen as more 'difficult'.

Liens

The right to arrest a ship or take other action to obtain security for a claim, usually a debt, varies widely between different jurisdictions around the world and the detail is beyond the scope of this book. However, at its simplest, the legal systems of most countries recognise the right of someone with a claim against the owner of a ship to exercise some right of attachment over the ship, often referred to as a lien, to obtain security for the claim.

In most jurisdictions claims for crew wages, salvage, collision and similar enjoy the more favourable status of maritime liens which can usually only be extinguished by payment in full or by a court-ordered sale of the ship, in which case the lien transfers to the sale proceeds.

Liens, maritime liens, mortgages and other forms of restriction on, or attachment of, property are complicated and dealing with them invariably requires specialist local legal advice.

Dispute resolution

In the early days of shipping, when two parties had a dispute they could not resolve they went to a trusted third party who would attempt to bring them together by persuasion – this was often the entity which today we call a ship broker. As commerce became more complex and specialised, a few senior shipbrokers active in London's shipping exchange (the Baltic Exchange) became acknowledged as 'wise heads' who could unravel the complex issues and would give an arbitrary judgment as to who was at fault and to what extent. This would be accepted by both parties in dispute. For many of us in shipping, it is a shame that we have lost this cheap, quick, and what was generally seen as a fair system for resolving disputes.

Mediation

This is the modern version of the trusted third party. Mediation is a form of alternative dispute resolution (ADR). It is a very cost-effective way to find a resolution to a contractual dispute but can only work if both parties genuinely want to settle. Both parties agree to appoint a mediator who, for a fee, will explore the details of the dispute and the position of each of the parties in dispute, and will endeavour to bring them to a point where they can agree on a settlement.

The mediator's proposal is not binding on the parties involved; it has to be their decision to settle.

Arbitration

This is the modern version of the 'wise heads'. It has become a very formal process and is frequently included as the selected method of dispute resolution in contracts.

In the marine sector, the majority of arbitrations are conducted under the rules of the London Maritime Arbitrators Association (LMAA), the Society of Marine Arbitrators in New York (SMA) or the Singapore Chamber of Maritime Arbitration (SCMA).

The simplest arbitration involves a single arbitrator jointly appointed by both parties who will rely solely on written submissions and then makes his judgment (award). The award will identify who has to pay, what and to whom. The award is binding on all parties involved and may not be appealed (except in very limited circumstances).

Most arbitrations involve each side of the dispute appointing an arbitrator; these two arbitrators then select a third to chair a tribunal. This will usually proceed through lodging written submissions and documentary evidence to a formal hearing, and there will usually be solicitors, barristers, witnesses and experts who will give opinions. The procedure can be lengthy and may become very expensive.

After considering the evidence and the arguments, the tribunal will publish its award, which will state who is to do what and, usually but not always, who is to pay what to whom. The award is final and may only be appealed in very limited circumstances. In the last few decades, arbitration has become as expensive as court action but is still the preferred solution in the maritime industry. In general, the award is confidential and this process seems to have found favour as the maritime industry does not like to 'wash its dirty linen' in public. Another factor favouring arbitration over court proceedings is that by reason of the New York Convention, it is generally easier to enforce an arbitration award in a foreign court than it is to enforce a judgment of a court of one country in the courts of another country.

Court

Using the courts to resolve disputes is one of the prime functions of commercial law. The procedure follows that of a full arbitration hearing with the exception being that the parties in dispute do not choose the judge. In some jurisdictions, England for example, there can be advantages over arbitration in terms of speed, the ability to 'join' other parties in the court proceedings and the power of the court to grant injunctions. However, a court decision can be subject to appeal to a higher court, adding to cost and slowing down the time taken to obtain a final decision. The judgment will also be a matter of public record. The choice of applicable law and the jurisdiction will usually be part of the contract. However, this can be influenced by other factors and, inevitably, the courts of some jurisdictions are more efficient and commercially minded than others.

Glossary

A

AA
Always Afloat.
A contract term requiring that the vessel does not rest on the ground. In some ports the ship is aground when approaching or at berth.

AAR
Against All Risks (insurance clause).

AASA
Always Afloat or Safely Aground. See above *Always Afloat.* Used where a vessel will be aground on a soft seabed during the cargo operation, settling aground as the tide goes out and refloating when the tide comes in. Only used for coastal trade ships.

ABAFT
A point beyond the midpoint of a ship's length, towards the rear or stern.

ABANDON
A proceeding wherein a shipper/consignee seeks authority to abandon all or parts of its cargo.

ABATEMENT
A discount allowed for damage or overcharge in the payment of a bill.

ABOARD
Referring to cargo being put, or laden, onto a means of conveyance.

ACCOMMODATION LADDER
A hinged set of steps lowered from the deck of the ship to provide access between quayside and the vessel.

ACT OF GOD
An act beyond human control, such as lightning, flood or earthquake.

ADMIRALTY (ADM)
Refers to marine matters such as an Admiralty Court.

ADVENTURE
A term used in some insurance policies to mean a voyage or a shipment.

AFT
Movement towards the stern (back end) of a ship.

AGENT (AGT)
A person authorised to transact business for, and in the name of, another person or company.

ALONGSIDE
A phrase referring to the side of a ship. Goods delivered 'alongside' are to be placed on the dock or barge within reach of the transport ship's tackle so that they can be loaded.

AMIDSHIPS
Midway between bow and stern.

APPARENT GOOD ORDER
When freight appears to be free of damage so far as a general survey can determine.

ASSIGNMENT
A term commonly used in connection with a bill of lading. It involves the transfer of rights, title and interest in order to assign goods by endorsing the bill of lading.

ASTERN
Behind a vessel.
Move in a reverse direction.

ATDNSHINC
Any time day or night Sundays and Holidays included. A chartering term referring to when a vessel will work.

ATHWARTSHIPS
A direction across the width of a vessel.

AUTOMATIC IDENTIFICATION SYSTEM (AIS)
A system used by ships and Vessel Traffic Service (VTS) principally for the identification and the locating of vessels. AIS provides a means for ships to electronically exchange ship data, including identification, position, course and speed, with other nearby ships and VTS stations.

AWWL
Always within institute warranties limits (for insurance purposes).

BB
Abbreviation for:

    Ballast bonus:

    A special payment above the chartering price when the ship has to sail a long way on ballast to reach the loading port.

    Bareboat:

A method of chartering the ship, leaving the charterer with almost all the responsibilities of the owner.

BACKHAUL
To haul a shipment back over part of a route it has already travelled.

BANK GUARANTEE
Guarantee issued by a bank to a carrier to be used in lieu of a lost or misplaced original negotiable bill of lading.

BARRATRY
An act committed by the Master or mariners of a vessel, for some unlawful or fraudulent purpose, contrary to their duty to the owners, whereby the latter sustain injury. It may include negligence, if so gross as to evidence fraud.

BARREL (BBL)
A term of measurement of oil in the United States referring to 42 US gallons of liquid at 60°F.

BEAM
The width of a ship.

BENEFICIARY
Entity to whom money is payable.
The entity for whom a letter of credit is issued.
The seller and the drawer of a draft.

BILL OF LADING (B/L)
A document that establishes the terms of a contract between a shipper and a transportation company. It serves as a document of title, a contract of carriage and a receipt for goods.

BLOCK STOWAGE
Stowing cargo destined for a specific location close together to avoid unnecessary cargo movement.

BLOCKING (OR BRACING)
Wood or metal supports to keep shipments in place to prevent cargo shifting. See also *Dunnage*.

BOARD
To gain access to a vessel.

BOARD FEET
The basic unit of measurement for lumber. One board foot is equal to a one-inch board, 12 inches wide and 1 foot (ft) long. Thus, a board 10-feet long, 12-inches wide, and 1-inch thick contains 10 board feet.

BOAT
A relatively small, usually open craft/vessel. A small, often open vessel for travelling on water. An inland vessel of any size.

BONDED WAREHOUSE
A warehouse authorised by Customs authorities for storage of goods on which payment of duties is deferred until the goods are removed.

BOW
The front of a vessel.

BREAK BULK
To unload and distribute a portion or all of the contents of container, trailer, or ship.
Packaged cargo that is not containerised.

BROKEN STOWAGE
The loss of space caused by irregularity in the shape of packages.
Any void or empty space in a vessel or container not occupied by cargo.

BROKER
A person who arranges for transportation of loads for a percentage of the revenue from the load.

BROKERAGE
Freight forwarder/broker compensation as specified by ocean tariff or contract.

BULK CARGO
Not in packages or containers; shipped loose in the hold of a ship. Grain, coal and sulphur are usually bulk freight.

BULK FREIGHT CONTAINER
A container with a discharge hatch in the front wall; allows bulk commodities to be carried.

BULKHEAD
A partition separating one part of a ship, freight car, aircraft or truck from another part.

BUNKER ADJUSTMENT FACTOR (BAF)
Used to compensate steamship lines for fluctuating fuel costs.

BUNKERS
A maritime term referring to fuel used onboard the ship. In the past, fuel coal stowage areas onboard a vessel were called bunkers.

CABOTAGE
Water transportation term applicable to shipments between ports of a nation; commonly refers to coastwise or inter-coastal navigation or trade. Many nations have cabotage laws which require national Flag vessels to provide domestic inter-port service.

CAPESIZE VESSEL
A dry bulk vessel whose beam precludes passage via the Panama Canal and thus compels it to pass around Cape Horn or the Cape of Good Hope.

CARGO
Freight loaded into a ship.

CARGO MANIFEST
A manifest that lists all cargo carried on a specific vessel voyage.

CARGO TONNAGE
Most ocean freight is billed on the basis of weight or measurement tons (W/M). Weight tons can be expressed in short tons of 2,000 pounds (lbs), long tons of 2,240 lbs or tonnes of 1,000 kilogrammes (kg) (2,204.62 lbs).
Measurement tons are usually expressed as cargo measurement of 40 ft^3 (1.12 cubic metres (m^3)).

CARNET
A Customs document permitting the holder to temporarily carry or send merchandise into certain foreign countries (for display, demonstration or similar purposes) without paying duties or posting bonds.
Any of various Customs documents required for crossing some international borders.

CARRIER
Any person or entity who, in a contract of carriage, undertakes to perform or to procure the performance of carriage by rail, road, sea, air, inland waterway or by a combination of such modes.

CENTRE OF GRAVITY
The point of equilibrium of the total weight of a container ship, truck, train or a piece of cargo.

CERTIFICATE OF ORIGIN
A certified document showing the origin of goods; used in international commerce.

CHARTER PARTY
A written contract between the owner of a vessel and the entity desiring to employ the vessel (charterer); sets forth the terms of the arrangement, such as duration of agreement, freight rate and ports involved in the trip.

CHOCK
A piece of wood or other material placed at the side of cargo to prevent rolling or moving sideways.

CLAIM
A demand made upon a transportation line for payment on account of a loss sustained through its alleged negligence.

CLASSIFICATION RATING
The designation provided in a classification by which a class rate is determined.

CLASSIFICATION SOCIETY
An organisation maintained for the surveying and classing of ships so that insurance underwriters and others may know the quality and condition of the vessels offered for insurance or employment.

CLEAN BILL OF LADING
A receipt for goods issued by a carrier with an indication that the goods were received in 'apparent good order and condition', without damage or other irregularities. If no notation or exception is made, the B/L is assumed to be 'clean'.

CLEAT
A strip of wood or metal used to afford additional strength, to prevent warping, or to hold in place.

CM
Abbreviation for cubic metre.

CM
Abbreviation for centimetre.

COASTWISE
Water transportation along the coast.

COGSA
Carriage of Goods by Sea Act. This exists in many jurisdictions and governs the rights and responsibilities between shippers of cargo and shipowners regarding ocean shipments.

COMMODITY
Article shipped. For dangerous and hazardous cargo, the correct commodity identification is critical.

COMMON CARRIER
A transportation company which provides services to the general public at published rates.

COMMON LAW
Law that derives its force and authority from precedent, custom and usage rather than from statutes, particularly with reference to the laws of England and the United States.

COMPANY SECURITY OFFICER
This is the person designated by a company for ensuring that a ship security assessment is carried out and that a ship security plan is developed, submitted for approval and thereafter implemented and maintained for liaison with port facility security officers and the ship security officer.

CONCEALED DAMAGE
Damage that is not evident from viewing an unopened package.

CONFERENCE
An association of shipowners operating on the same trade route who operate under collective conditions and agree on tariff rates.

CONSIGNEE
A person or company to whom commodities are shipped.

CONTAINER MANIFEST
Document showing contents and loading sequence, point of origin, and point of destination for a container. Vessels are required by law to carry such a document for each container carried.

CONTAINER TERMINAL
An area designated for the stowage of cargoes in a container; usually accessible by truck, railroad and marine transportation. Here, containers are picked up, dropped off, maintained and housed.

CONTRABAND
Cargo that is prohibited.

CONTRACT
A legally binding agreement between two or more persons/organisations to carry out reciprocal obligations or value.

CONTROLLED ATMOSPHERE
Sophisticated, computer-controlled systems that manage the mixtures of gases within a container throughout an intermodal journey, thereby reducing decay.

CORRESPONDENT BANK
A bank that, in its own country, handles the business of a foreign bank.

COST AND INSURANCE (CI)
A price that includes the cost of the goods, the marine insurance and all transportation charges, except the ocean freight, to the named point of destination.

COST, INSURANCE AND FREIGHT (CIF)
Cost of goods, marine insurance and all transportation (freight) charges are paid to the foreign point of delivery by the seller.

CUBE OUT
When a container or vessel has reached its volumetric capacity before its permitted weight limit.

CUBIC METRE (CU)
Can be abbreviated to CBM or CM. A unit of volume measurement.

CURRENCY ADJUSTMENT FACTOR (CAF)
A charge, expressed as a percentage of a base rate, that is applied to compensate ocean carriers of currency fluctuations.

CUSTOMS
Government agency charged with enforcing the rules passed to protect the country's import and export revenues.

CUSTOMS BONDED WAREHOUSE
A warehouse authorised by Customs to receive duty-free merchandise.

CUSTOMS OF THE PORT (COP)
A phrase often included in charter parties and freight contracts referring to local rules and practices which may impact upon the costs borne by the various parties.

D

DEADWEIGHT TONNAGE (DWT)
The number of tonnes of 2,240 lbs that a vessel can transport of cargo, stores and bunker fuel. It is the difference between the number of tons of water a vessel displaces 'light' and the number of tons it displaces when submerged to the 'load line'.

DEMURRAGE
A penalty charge against shippers or consignees for delaying the carrier's equipment or vessel beyond the allowed free time. The free time and demurrage charges are set forth in the charter party or freight tariff. In legal terms, liquidated damages; the shipowner has only to demonstrate the time delay, it does not have to itemise damage caused by the delay.
See also *Detention and Per Diem*.

DESPATCH
An incentive payment paid by the vessel to the charterer for loading and unloading the cargo faster than agreed. Usually negotiated only in charter parties. Also called 'dispatch'.

DESTINATION
The place to which a shipment is consigned.

DETENTION
A penalty charge against shippers or consignees for delaying a carrier's equipment beyond allowed time. Demurrage applies to cargo; detention applies to equipment.

DISPATCH
See *Despatch*.

DISPLACEMENT
The weight, in tons of 2,240 lbs or tons of 1,000 kg, of the vessel and its contents.

DIVERSION
A change made either in the route of a shipment in transit or of the entire ship.

DOCK FOR SHIPS
A cargo handling area parallel to the shoreline where a vessel normally ties up.

DOCKAGE
Refers to the charge assessed against the vessel for berthing at the facility or for mooring to a vessel so berthed.

DRAUGHT
The depth that the hull of a ship is beneath the surface of the water. This can be draught 'ford' (at the bow), draught 'aft' (at the stern) or draught 'amidship' (halfway along the hull).

DRY CARGO
Cargo that is not liquid and normally does not require temperature control.

DUMPING
Attempting to import merchandise into a country at a price less than the fair market value, usually through subsidy by exporting country.

DUNNAGE
Any material or objects utilised to protect cargo. Examples of dunnage are blocks, boards, burlap and paper.

E

EMISSION CONTROL AREA (ECA)
A geographical area of the sea which has additional restrictions on atmospheric pollution, designated as part of MARPOL Annex VI.

ETA
Estimated time of arrival.

ETC
Estimated time of completion.

ETD
Estimated time of departure.

ETR
Estimated time of readiness.

ETS
Estimated time of sailing.

EXPORT
Shipment of goods to another country.

EXPORT LICENCE
A government document which permits the licensee to engage in the export of designated goods to certain destinations.

F

FCL
Abbreviation for 'full container load'.

FD
Abbreviation for 'free discharge.

FEEDER SERVICE
Cargo to/from regional ports transferred to/from a central hub port for a long-haul ocean voyage.

FEEDER VESSEL
A short sea vessel which transfers cargo between a central hub port and smaller spoke ports.

FEU
Abbreviation for forty-foot equivalent unit. Refers to a container size standard of 40 feet. Two twenty-foot containers (TEU) equal one FEU.

FIO
Abbreviation for 'free in and out' (where voyage charterer pays for the expenses of loading and discharge).

FIXED COSTS
Costs that do not vary with the level of activity. Some fixed costs continue even if no cargo is carried. Vessel operating costs, vessel finance, insurance, terminal leases, rent and property taxes are fixed costs.

FORCE MAJEURE
The title of a common clause in contracts, exempting the parties for non-fulfilment of their obligations as a result of conditions beyond their control, such as earthquakes, floods or war.

FOREIGN TRADE ZONE
A free port in a country divorced from Customs authority but under government control. Merchandise, except that which is prohibited, may be stored in the zone without being subject to import duty regulations.

FREE ALONGSIDE SHIP (FAS)
The seller must deliver the goods to a pier and place them within reach of the ship's loading equipment. See *Terms of Sale*.

FREE ONBOARD
See *Terms of Sale*.

FREE PORT
A restricted area at a seaport for the handling of duty-exempted imported goods.

FREE TIME
The amount of time that a carrier's equipment may be used without incurring additional charges. (See *Storage, Demurrage* or *Per Diem.*)

FREE TRADE ZONE
A port designated by the government of a country for duty-free entry of any non-prohibited goods. Merchandise may be stored, displayed, used for manufacturing, etc. within the zone and re-exported without the imposition of duties.

FREIGHT
Refers to either the cargo carried or the charges assessed for carriage of the cargo.

FREIGHT FORWARDER
An entity whose business is to act as an agent on behalf of the shipper. A freight forwarder frequently makes the booking reservation.

FULL AND DOWN
An expression to describe a loaded vessel carrying cargoes of such a volume and weight that it fills all the vessel's spaces and also brings her down to her tonnage load line. A rare, but optimum, revenue condition for a vessel operator.

GANGWAY
Ladder or ramp providing a means of access from the quayside onto the vessel.

GREENWICH MEAN TIME (GMT)
A time system originally based on the time at 0 degrees of Longitude as observed by the observatory at Greenwich in the United Kingdom. It is now adjusted to deal with the variation in the speed of rotation of the earth, which is why it is called Greenwich Mean Time, rather than Greenwich Time.

GROSS TONNAGE (GT)
Applies to vessels, not to cargo (0.2+0.02 logV), where V is the volume in cubic metres of all enclosed spaces on the vessel. Since 1994, it has replaced gross registered tonnage. An approximate conversion ratio is 1 net ton (NT) = 1.7 gross ton (GT) and 1 GT = 1.5 deadweight tonne (DWT).

GROSS WEIGHT
Entire weight of goods, packaging and freight car or container, ready for shipment. Generally, 80,000 lbs maximum container, cargo and tractor for highway transport.

H

HAGUE RULES, THE
A multilateral maritime treaty adopted in 1921 (at The Hague, Netherlands). Standardises liability of an international carrier under the Ocean bill of lading. Establishes a legal 'floor' for bill of lading.

HAGUE-VISBY RULES, THE
Additional protocols to The Hague rules from 1968 and 1979.

HAMBURG RULES, THE.
A maritime treaty adopted in 1978 to cover the liability of an international carrier under the Ocean bill of lading.

HANDYMAX VESSEL
A dry bulk vessel of 35,000-49,000 DWT (Note that a 'Handy' drybulk carrier is from 10,000-34,000 DWT). A Handymax tanker is a liquid bulk carrier of 10,000 -60,000 DWT.

HARBOUR
Any place to which ships may resort for shelter, or to load or unload passengers or goods, or to obtain fuel, water, or supplies. This term applies to such places whether proclaimed public or not and whether natural or artificial.

HARBOUR MASTER
An official responsible for the construction, maintenance, operation, regulation, enforcement, administration and management pertaining to marinas, ports and harbours.

HATCH
The opening in the deck of a vessel; gives access to the cargo hold.

HAZMAT
An industry abbreviation for hazardous material.

HEAVY-LIFT CHARGE
A charge made for lifting articles too heavy to be lifted by a ship's normal tackle.

HOPPER BARGE
A barge which loads material dumped into it by a dredger and discharges the cargo through the bottom.

I

IMDG CODE
International Maritime Dangerous Goods Code. The regulations published by the IMO for transporting hazardous materials internationally.

IMPORT
To receive goods from a foreign country.

IMPORT LICENCE
A document required and issued by some national governments authorising the importation of goods.

IN BOND
Cargo moving under Customs' control where duty has not yet been paid.

INCOTERMS
The recognised abbreviation for the International Chamber of Commerce Terms of Sale. These terms were last amended, effective from January 2011.

INHERENT VICE
An insurance term referring to any defect or other characteristic of a product that could result in damage to the product without external cause (for example, instability in a chemical that could cause it to explode spontaneously). Insurance policies may exclude inherent vice losses.

INLAND CARRIER
A transportation line that hauls export or import traffic between ports and inland points.

INSPECTION CERTIFICATE
A certificate issued by an independent agent or firm attesting to the quality and/or quantity of the merchandise being shipped. Such a certificate is usually required in a letter of credit for commodity shipments.

INSULATED CONTAINER
A container insulated on the walls, roof, floor, and doors to reduce the effect of external temperatures on the cargo.

INSULATED CONTAINER TANK
The frame of a container constructed to hold one or more thermally insulated tanks for liquids.

INSURANCE, GENERAL AVERAGE
In water transportation, the deliberate sacrifice of cargo to make the vessel safe for the remaining cargo. Those sharing in the spared cargo proportionately cover the loss.

INSURANCE, PARTICULAR AVERAGE
A marine insurance term which refers to partial loss on an individual shipment from one of the perils insured against, regardless of the balance of the cargo. Particular average insurance can usually be obtained, but the loss must be in excess of a certain percentage of the insured value of the shipment, usually 3%-5%, before a claim will be allowed by the company.

INTERCOASTAL
Water service between two coasts; in the United States, this usually refers to water service between the Atlantic and Pacific or Gulf Coasts.

INTERMODAL
Used to denote movements of cargo containers interchangeably between transport modes, i.e., motor, rail, water, and air carriers, and where the equipment is compatible within the multiple systems.

INTERNATIONAL ORGANIZATION FOR STANDARDIZATION (ISO)
The International Organization for Standardization deals in standards of all sorts, ranging from documentation to equipment packaging and labelling.

INTERNATIONAL SHIP AND PORT FACILITY SECURITY (ISPS) CODE
This is an amendment to the Safety of Life at Sea (SOLAS) Convention (1974/1988) on minimum security arrangements for ships, ports and government agencies. It came into force in 2004, and it prescribes responsibilities to governments, shipping companies, shipboard personnel, and port/facility personnel to 'detect security threats and take preventative measures against security incidents affecting ships or port facilities used in international trade'.

IRREVOCABLE LETTER OF CREDIT
Letter of credit in which the specified payment is guaranteed by the bank if all terms and conditions are met by the drawee and which cannot be revoked without joint agreement of both the buyer and the seller.

ISSUING BANK
A bank that opens a straight or negotiable letter of credit and assumes the obligation to pay the bank or beneficiary if the documents presented are in accordance with the terms of the letter of credit.

J

JACKET
A wooden or fibre cover placed around containers such as cans and bottles.

JACOB'S LADDER
A simple rope ladder suspended from the side of a vessel and used for boarding.

JETTISON
Act of throwing cargo or equipment (jetsam) overboard when a ship is in danger.

JUST IN TIME (JIT)
In this method of inventory control, warehousing is minimal or non-existent; the container is the movable warehouse and must arrive 'just in time'; not too early nor too late.

K

KILOGRAMME
1,000 grammes or 2,2046 lbs.

KNOCKED DOWN (KD)
Articles which are taken apart to reduce the cubic footage displaced or to make a better shipping unit and are to be re-assembled.

KNOT
One nautical mile (6,076 ft or 1,852 m) per hour. In the days of sail, speed was measured by tossing overboard a log which was secured by a line. Knots were tied into the line at intervals of approximately 6 feet. The number of knots measured was then compared against time required to travel the distance of 1,000 knots in the line.

L

LAYCAN
Laydays/Cancelling (date).
Range of dates within which the hire contract must start.

LAYDAYS
Specific time period (days) during which the vessel must arrive at the loading port ready for loading.

LAYTIME
Time allowed for the vessel's cargo to be loaded/discharged without incurring demurrage.

LETTER OF CREDIT (LC)
A document, issued by a bank per instructions by a buyer of goods, authorising the seller to draw a specified sum of money under specified terms; usually the receipt by the bank of certain documents within a given time.

Irrevocable LC:

An instrument that, once established, cannot be modified or cancelled without the agreement of all parties concerned.

Revolving LC:

An irrevocable letter issued for a specific amount; renews itself for the same amount over a given period.

LETTER OF INDEMNITY
In order to obtain a clean bill of lading, the shipper signs a letter of indemnity to the carrier on the basis of which may be obtained the clean bill of lading, although the dock or mate's receipt showed that the shipment was damaged or in bad condition.

LIEN
A legal claim upon goods for the satisfaction of some debt or duty.

LIGHTERING
A vessel discharges part of its cargo at anchor into a lighter to reduce the vessel's draught so it can then get alongside a pier.

LIGHTER
An open or covered barge towed by a tugboat and used mainly in harbours and inland waterways to carry cargo to/from alongside a vessel.

LINER
A vessel advertising sailings on a specified trade route on a regular basis. It is not necessary that every named port be called on every voyage.

LIQUEFIED NATURAL GAS (LNG)
Natural gas will liquefy at a temperature of approximately -259°F or -160°C at atmospheric pressure. One cubic foot of liquefied gas will expand to approximately 600 cubic feet of gas at atmospheric pressure.

LIST
The amount in degrees that a vessel tilts from the vertical.

LITRE
1.06 liquid US quarts, or 33.9 fluid ounces.

LLOYD'S REGISTER
An organisation maintained for the surveying and classing of ships so that insurance underwriters and others may know the quality and condition of the vessels offered for insurance or employment.

LNGC (LNG CARRIER)
An ocean-going ship specially constructed to carry LNG in tanks at -160°C. Current average carrying capacity of LNGCs is 125,000 m³. Many LNGCs currently under construction or on order are in the 210,000-215,000 m³ range.

LOAD LINE
The waterline corresponding to the maximum draught to which a vessel is permitted to load, either by freeboard regulations, the conditions of classification, or the conditions of service. See also *Plimsoll mark*.

LONG TON
2,240 lbs.

LONGSHOREMAN
Individual employed in a port to load and unload ships. Also called a stevedore.

M

MALPRACTICE
A carrier giving a customer illegal preference to attract cargo. This can take the form of a money refund (rebate); using lower figures than actual for the assessment of freight charges (undercubing); misdeclaration of the commodity

shipped to allow the assessment of a lower tariff rate; waiving published tariff charges for demurrage, CFS handling or equalisation; providing specialised equipment to a shipper to the detriment of other shippers, etc.

MANIFEST
Document that lists in detail all the bills of lading issued by a carrier or its agent or master for a specific voyage. A detailed summary of the total cargo of a vessel. Used principally for Customs' purposes.

MARINE INSURANCE
Broadly, insurance covering loss or damage of goods at sea. Marine insurance (cargo) typically compensates the owner of merchandise for losses sustained from fire, shipwreck, etc., but excludes losses that can be recovered from the carrier. Marine insurance (Hull and Machinery) compensates the vessel owner for damage to, or loss of, the vessel.

MARLINESPIKE
A pointed metal spike used to separate strands of rope in splicing.

MARPOL
The International Convention for the Prevention of Pollution from Ships. It was designed to minimise pollution of the seas, including dumping, oil and exhaust pollution. It entered into force in 1983.

MATE'S RECEIPT
An archaic practice. An acknowledgement of cargo receipt signed by a mate of the vessel. The possessor of the mate's receipt is entitled to the bill of lading, in exchange for that receipt.

MBM
1,000 board feet. One MBM equals 2,265 CM.

MECHANICALLY VENTILATED CONTAINER
A container fitted with a means of forced air ventilation.

METRE
39.37 inches (approximately).

TONNE
2,204.6 lbs or 1,000 kg.

MILE
A unit equal to 5,280 ft on land. A nautical mile is 6,076.115 ft.

MT
Abbreviation for metric ton or tonne.

MTSA
The US *Maritime Transportation Security Act* of 2002 is designed to protect ports and waterways from terrorist attacks. The law is the US equivalent of the International Ship and Port Facility Security (ISPS) Code, and was fully

implemented on 1 July 2004. It requires vessels and port facilities to conduct vulnerability assessments and develop security plans that may include passenger, vehicle, and baggage screening procedures; security patrols; establishing restricted areas; personnel identification procedures; access control measures; and/or installation of surveillance equipment.

MULTIMODAL
Synonymous, for all practical purposes, with 'intermodal'.

MULTI-TANK CONTAINER
A container frame fitted to accommodate two or more separate tanks for liquids.

N

NAUTICAL MILE
Distance of one minute of longitude at the equator, approximately 6,076.115 ft. The metric equivalent is 1,852 m.

NEGOTIABLE INSTRUMENTS
A document of title (such as a draft, promissory note, check, or bill of lading) transferable from one person to another in good faith for a consideration. Non-negotiable bills of lading are known as 'straight consignment'. Negotiable bills are known as 'order b/ls'.

NET TARE WEIGHT
The weight of an empty cargo-carrying piece of equipment plus any fixtures permanently attached.

NET TONNAGE (NT)
The replacement, since 1994, for 'net register tonnage'; theoretically, the cargo capacity of the ship. Sometimes used to charge fees or taxes on a vessel. The formula is $(0.2+0.02 \log(Vc)) Vc (4d/3D)2$; for passenger ships, the following formula is added: $1.25 (GT+10,000)/10,000 (N1+(N2/10))$, where Vc is the volume of cargo holds, D is the distance between ship's bottom and the uppermost deck, d is the draught, N1 is the number of cabin passengers, and N2 is the number of deck passengers. 'Tonne' is figured as a 100 cubic foot tonne. An approximate conversion ratio is 1 NT = 1.7 GT and 1 GT = 1.5 DWT.

NET WEIGHT
Weight of the goods alone without any immediate wrappings, e.g., the weight of the contents of a tin can without the weight of the can.

NON-VESSEL OPERATING COMMON CARRIER (NVOCC)
A cargo consolidator in ocean trades who will buy space from a carrier and sub-sell it to smaller shippers. The NVOCC issues bills of lading, publishes tariffs and otherwise conducts itself as an ocean common carrier, except that it will not provide the actual ocean or intermodal service.

NOTICE OF READINESS (NOR)
Notice of readiness (when the ship is ready to load).

NRT
Net register tons see *Net tonnage*.
Theoretically, the cargo capacity of the ship. Sometimes used to charge fees or taxes on a vessel.

OPEN SEA
The water area of the open coast seaward of the ordinary low-water mark, or seaward of inland waters.

OPEN TOP CONTAINER
A container fitted with a solid removable roof, or with a tarpaulin roof, so the container can be loaded or unloaded from the top.

ORIGIN
Location where shipment begins its movement.

ORIGINAL BILL OF LADING (OBL)
A document which requires proper signatures for consummating carriage of contract. Must be marked as 'original' by the issuing carrier.

P&I
Abbreviation for 'Protection and Indemnity', an insurance term.

P&I CLUB
A mutual organisation which provides P&I cover to its members, the costs being met by all of the members of that club.

PALLET
A platform, with or without sides, on which a number of packages or pieces may be loaded to facilitate handling by a lift truck.

PANAMAX TANKER
A liquid cargo vessel of 50,000 to 70,000 DWT.

PANAMAX VESSEL
The largest size vessel able to traverse the Panama Canal (prior to its expansion). Maximum dimensions are: length 294.1 m (965 ft) width 32.3 m (106 ft); draught 12.0 m (39.5 ft) in tropical fresh water; height 57.91 m (190 ft) above the water.

PER DIEM
A charge, based on a fixed daily rate.

PERILS OF THE SEA
Those causes of loss for which the carrier is not legally liable; the elemental risks of ocean transport.

PIER
A structure perpendicular to the shoreline to which a vessel is secured for the purposes of loading and unloading cargo.

PLACE OF DELIVERY
A place where cargo leaves the care and custody of the carrier.

PLACE OF RECEIPT
A location where cargo enters the care and custody of the carrier.

PLIMSOLL MARK
A series of horizontal lines, corresponding to the seasons of the year and fresh or saltwater, painted on the outside of a ship marking the level which must remain above the surface of the water for the vessel's stability.

PORT
The left-hand side of the ship when facing the bow.

PROOF OF DELIVERY
A document required from the carrier or driver for proper payment.

POINT OF ORIGIN
The place at which a shipment is received by a carrier from the shipper.

PRATIQUE CERTIFICATE
Lifts temporary quarantine of a vessel; granted pratique by a port health officer.

PRE-COOLING
A process employed in the shipment of citrus fruits and other perishable commodities. The fruit is packed and placed in a cold room from which the heat is gradually extracted. The boxes of fruit are packed in containers that have been thoroughly cooled and transported through to destination without opening the doors.

PREPAID (PPD)
Freight charges paid by the consignor (shipper) prior to the release of the bills of lading by the carrier.

PRODUCT TANKER
A liquid cargo vessel of 10,000 to 60,000 DWT. Also referred to as a Handymax tanker. Often built with many segregated cargo tanks and thus sometimes called a parcel tanker.

PRO FORMA
A Latin term meaning 'for the sake of form'.

PRO FORMA INVOICE
An invoice provided by a supplier prior to the shipment of merchandise, informing the buyer of the kinds and quantities of goods to be sent, their value, and specifications (weight, size, etc.).

PRO RATA
A Latin term meaning 'in proportion'.

QUARANTINE
A restraint placed on an operation to protect the public against a health hazard. A ship may be quarantined so that it cannot leave a protected point. During the quarantine period, the Q flag (a solid yellow square-shaped flag) is hoisted.

QUOIN
A wedge-shaped piece of timber used to secure barrels against movement.

QUOTA
The quantity of goods that may be imported without restriction during a set period of time.

QUOTATION
An offer to sell goods at a stated price and under stated terms.

QUAY
A structure attached to land to which a vessel is moored. See also *Pier* and *Dock*.

REASONABLENESS
Under International Chamber of Commerce (ICC) and common law, the requirement that a rate not be higher than is necessary to reimburse the carrier for the actual cost of transporting the traffic and to allow a fair profit.

REBATE
A form of discounting or refunding that has the net effect of lowering the price.

RECONSIGNMENT
Changing the consignee or destination on a bill of lading while shipment is still in transit. Diversion has substantially the same meaning.

RECOURSE
A right claim against the guarantors of a loan or draft or bill of exchange.

RED LABEL
A label required on shipments of flammable articles.

REEFER
Refrigerated container.

RFP
Request for proposal.

RFQ
Request for quotation.

REMITTANCE
Funds sent by one entity to another as payment.

RESTRICTED ARTICLES
Articles handled only under certain conditions.

REVENUE TONNE (RT)
Billing unit in the shipping industry. One revenue ton equals the weight in tonnes or the volume in cubic metres, whichever is higher in terms of the freight.

RO-RO
A shortening of the term 'Roll-on Roll-off'. A method of ocean cargo service using a vessel with ramps which allows wheeled vehicles to be loaded and discharged without cranes. Also refers to any specialised vessel designed to carry Ro-Ro cargo.

ROTTERDAM RULES, THE
This convention aims to establish a modern, comprehensive, uniform legal regime governing the rights and obligations of shippers, carriers and consignees under a contract for door-to-door shipments that involve international sea transport. It was organised by the United Nations and was adopted in 2008.

SANCTION
An embargo imposed by a government against another country.

SEAWAYMAX VESSEL
The largest vessel that can transit the locks of the St Lawrence Seaway. Length is 226 m (740 ft); beam is 24 m (78 ft); draught is 7.92 m (26 ft).

SEAWORTHINESS
The fitness of a vessel for its intended use.

SHEX
Saturday and holidays excluded.

SHINC
Saturday and holidays included.

SHIP
(1) A vessel of considerable size for deep-water navigation.

(2) A sailing vessel having three or more square-rigged masts.

SHIP CHANDLER
An individual or company selling equipment and supplies for ships.

SHIP'S BELLS
These measure time onboard ship. One bell sounds for each half hour. One bell means 12:30, two bells mean 1:00, three bells mean 1:30, and so on until 4:00 (eight bells). At 4:30 the cycle begins again with one bell.

SHIP'S MANIFEST
A statement listing the particulars of all shipments loaded for a specified voyage.

SHIPMENT
The tender of one lot of cargo at one time from one shipper to one consignee on one bill of lading.

SHIP SECURITY OFFICER
This is the person onboard the vessel, accountable to the Master, designated by a company as responsible for the security of the ship, including implementation and maintenance of the ship security plan and for the liaison with the company security officer and the port facility security officers.

SHIP SECURITY PLAN
This is a plan developed to ensure the application of measures onboard the ship and designed to protect persons onboard, cargo, cargo transport units, ship's stores, or the ship from the risks of a security incident.

SHIP TYPES
Barge carriers: ships designed to carry barges; some are fitted to act as full container ships and can carry a varying number of barges and containers at the same time. At present, this class includes two types of vessel, LASH and Sea-Bee.

Bulk carriers: all vessels designed to carry bulk homogeneous cargo without mark and count, such as grain, fertilisers, ore and oil.

Combination passenger and cargo vessels: ships with a capacity for 13 or more passengers and any form of cargo or freight.

Freighters: breakbulk vessels, both refrigerated and unrefrigerated, container ships, partial container ships, Ro-Ro vessels, and barge carriers. A general cargo vessel designed to carry heterogeneous mark and count cargoes.

Full container ships: ships equipped with permanent container cells, with little or no space for other types of cargo.

General cargo carriers: breakbulk freighters, car carriers, livestock carriers, pallet carriers and timber carriers. A vessel designed to carry heterogeneous mark and count cargoes.

Partial container ships: multipurpose container ships where one or more but not all compartments are fitted with permanent container cells. Remaining compartments are used for other types of cargo.

Ro-Ro vessels: ships specially designed to carry wheeled containers or trailers using interior ramps. Includes all forms of car and truck carriers.

Tankers: ships fitted with tanks to carry liquid bulk cargo such as crude petroleum and petroleum products, chemicals, liquefied gases (LNG and LPG), wine and molasses.

SHIP'S TACKLE
All rigging, cranes, etc., utilised on a ship to load or unload cargo.

SHIPPER
The person or company who is usually the supplier or owner of commodities shipped. Also called consignor.

SHORE
A prop or support placed against or beneath anything to prevent sinking or sagging.

SHORT SEA SHIPPING
Short sea shipping means the movement of cargo by sea between ports situated in geographical Europe or between those ports situated in non-European countries having a coastline on the enclosed seas bordering Europe (Baltic, Mediterranean and Black).

SHORT TONNE (ST)
A weight unit of measure equal to 2,000 lbs.

SLING
A wire or rope contrivance placed around cargo and used to load or discharge it to/from a vessel.

SLIP
A vessel's berth between two piers.

SOLAS
International Convention for the Safety of Life at Sea. It ensures that ships flagged by signatory States comply with minimum safety standards in construction, equipment and operation. It entered into force in 1965.

SSHEX
Abbreviation for Saturdays, Sundays and holidays excepted. Refers to loading and discharging of cargo as agreed to in the charter party. This indicates when time does not count in the calculation of demurrage and despatch.

STABILITY
The force that holds a vessel upright or returns it to an upright position if keeled over. Weight in the lower hold increases stability. A vessel is 'stiff' if it has high

stability, 'tender' if it has low stability. In a ship, stability is indicated by several characteristics. Initial stability is measured by the metacentric height; also known as 'GM'. If the GM is low, the vessel makes long slow rolls, and is considered tender. When the GM is too high, the vessel is considered stiff, and may return violently to the upright position when rolling, with possible damage to cargo and injury to passengers and crew. Other stability considerations include the vessel's range of stability, maximum righting arm, and the angle of heel at which the maximum righting arm occurs.

STARBOARD
The right-side of a ship when facing the bow.

STCW
The International Convention on Standards of Training, Certification and Watchkeeping for Seafarers. It sets qualification standards for masters, officers and watch personnel on seagoing merchant ships. It entered into force in 1984.

STEM
Another name for the bow.

STERN
The back end of a vessel.

STEVEDORE
Individual or firm that employs longshoremen and who contracts them to load or unload the ship.

STOWAGE
A marine term referring to loading freight into ships' holds.

SUEZMAX TANKER
A tanker of 120,000 to 199,000 DWT.

SULPHUR EMISSION CONTROL AREA (SECA)
Sulphur emission control area. A geographical area of the sea which has additional restrictions on atmospheric pollution, designated as part of MARPOL Annex VI. Now being replaced by ECA as additional restrictions come into force.

SURCHARGE
An extra or additional charge.

SURTAX
An additional extra tax.

T

TARE WEIGHT
In railcar or container shipments, the weight of the empty railcar or empty container.

TARIFF
A publication setting forth the charges, rates and rules of transportation companies.

TEMPERATURE RECORDER
A device to record temperature in a container while cargo is en route.

TENDER
The offer of goods for transportation or the offer to place cars or containers for loading or unloading.

TERMINAL
An assigned area in which containers are prepared for loading into a vessel, train, truck or aircraft or are stacked immediately after discharge from the vessel, train, truck or aircraft.

TERMINAL CHARGE
A charge made for a service performed in a carrier's terminal area.

TERMS OF SALE
The point at which sellers have fulfilled their obligations so the goods, in a legal sense, could be said to have been delivered to the buyer. They are shorthand expressions that set out the rights and obligations of each party when it comes to transporting the goods.

TEU
Abbreviation for twenty-foot equivalent unit.

TIME CHARTER
A contract for leasing between the shipowner and the lessee. It would state, for example, the duration of the lease in years or voyages.

TO BE NOMINATED (TBN)
When the name of a ship, port or agent is still unknown.

TONNE-MILE
A unit used in comparing freight earnings or expenses. The amount earned from the cost of hauling a tonne of freight one mile. The movement of a tonne of freight one mile.

TOWAGE
The charge made for towing a vessel.

TRAMP LINE
An ocean carrier company operating vessels not on regular runs or schedules. They call at any port where cargo may be available.

TRANSSHIP
To transfer goods from one transportation line to another, or from one ship to another.

TRANSSHIPMENT PORT
A place where cargo is transferred to another carrier.

TURNAROUND
In water transportation, the time it takes between the arrival of a vessel and its departure.

TWIST LOCKS
A set of four twistable bayonet type shear keys used as part of a spreader to pick up a container or as part of a chassis to secure the containers.

 U

ULCC
Ultra large crude carrier. A tanker in excess of 320,000 DWT.

ULLAGE
The space not filled with liquid in a drum or tank.

UNCLOS
The United Nations Convention on the Law of the Sea which was signed in 1982 and entered into force in 1994. It defines the rights and responsibilities of nations in their use of the world's oceans, establishing guidelines for businesses, the environment and the management of marine natural resources.

UNDERWAY
A vessel is underway when it is not at anchor, made fast to the shore, or aground.

UNIT LOAD
Packages loaded on a pallet, in a crate or any other way that enables them to be handled at one time as a unit.

UNITISATION
The consolidation of a quantity of individual items into one large shipping unit for easier handling.
Loading one or more large items of cargo onto a single piece of equipment, such as a pallet.

UNLOADING
Removal of a shipment from a vessel.

V

VARIABLE COST
Costs that vary directly with the level of activity within a short time. Examples include costs of fuel, canal dues, port charges, stevedoring in some ports, and short-term equipment leases. For business analysis, all costs are either defined as variable or fixed. For a business to break even, all fixed costs must be covered.

To make a profit, all variable and fixed costs must be recovered plus an additional amount earned.

VLCC
Very large crude carrier. A tanker of 200,000 - 319,000 DWT. It can carry about 2 million barrels of crude oil.

WAR RISK
Insurance cover for loss of goods resulting from any act of war.

WAREHOUSE
A place for the reception, delivery, consolidation, distribution and storage of goods/cargo.

WAREHOUSE ENTRY
A document that identifies goods imported when placed in a bonded warehouse. The duty is not imposed on the products while in the warehouse but will be collected when they are withdrawn for delivery or consumption.

WAYBILL (WB)
A document prepared by a transportation line at the point of a shipment; shows the point of the origin, destination, route, consignor, consignee, description of shipment and amount charged for the transportation service. It is forwarded with the shipment or sent by mail to the agent at the transfer point or waybill destination. Unlike a bill of lading, a waybill is *not* a document of title.

WEIGHT CARGO
A cargo on which the transportation charge is assessed on the basis of weight.

Weights and Measures/Measurement tonne: 40 ft^3 or 1 m^3

Net tonne/short tonne –2,000 lbs

Gross ton/long ton –2,240 lbs

Tonne/kilo ton –2,204.6 lbs

Cubic metre –35.314 ft^3.

WHARF
A structure built on the shore of a harbour extending into deep water so that vessels may lie alongside. See also *Dock* and *Pier*.

WHARFAGE
Charge assessed by a pier or dock owner against freight handled over the pier or dock or against a steamship company using the pier or dock.

WIBON
Whether in berth or not.

WITHOUT RECOURSE
A phrase preceding the signature of a drawer or endorser of a negotiable instrument; signifies that the instrument is passed onto subsequent holders without any liability to the endorser in the event of non-payment or non-delivery.

WWD
Weather working days.

YORK-ANTWERP RULES OF 1974
Established the standard basis for adjusting General Average and stated the rules for adjusting claims.

ZULU TIME
Time based on Greenwich Mean Time (GMT) (now generally replaced by coordinated universal time (UTC). The definition of UTC is much more precise than GMT but for most purposes they can be regarded as the same.

Appendix 1 - Where to go for help

BIMCO – Baltic and International Maritime Council (BIMCO)

www.bimco.org

BIMCO is a shipping association providing a wide range of services to its global membership of stakeholders who have vested interests in the shipping industry, including shipowners, operators, managers, brokers and agents. The association's main objective is to facilitate the commercial operations of its membership by means of developing standard contracts and clauses, and providing quality information, advice, and education.

CLIA – Cruise Lines International Association

www.cruising.org

The non-profit CLIA is North America's largest global cruise industry organisation in terms of cruise line, industry supplier, and travel agency membership.

IACS – International Association of Classification Societies

www.iacs.org.uk

Dedicated to safe ships and clean seas, IACS contributes to maritime safety and regulation through technical support, compliance verification and research and development. More than 90% of the world's cargo-carrying tonnage is covered by the design, construction and through-life compliance rules and standards set by the 13 member societies of IACS.

IAPH – International Association of Ports and Harbors

www.iaphworldports.org

IAPH has developed into a global alliance of ports, representing today some 200 ports in 85 countries. The member ports together handle well over 60% of the world's seaborne trade and nearly 80% of the world's container traffic. It is a non-profit-making and non-governmental organisation (NGO) headquartered in Tokyo, Japan.

IBIA – International Bunker Industry Association

www.ibia.net

IBIA was conceived in October 1992 by eight members of the industry. Since then, it has expanded steadily with a worldwide membership comprising shipowners, charterers, bunker suppliers, traders, brokers, barging companies, storage companies, surveyors, port authorities, credit reporting companies, lawyers, P&I clubs, equipment manufacturers, shipping journalists and marine consultants. Membership currently stands at over 600 members from 66 countries.

ICS – Institute of Chartered Shipbrokers

www.ics.org.uk

With 25 branches and 17 distance learning centres around the world, the members of the ICS are part of an internationally recognised network of shipping professionals who not only work towards high professional ethical standards of trust, but who also have proven knowledge, competence and understanding of the broad spectrum of shipping business.

ICS – International Chamber of Shipping

www.ics-shipping.org

The ICS is the principal international trade association for merchant shipowners and operators, representing all sectors and trades and over 80% of the world merchant fleet.

IHMA – International Harbour Masters' Association

www.harbourmaster.org

The International Harbour Masters' Association is a non-profit making professional body that unites harbour masters around the world. With 200 members in 40 countries, the Association strives to bring together all those who hold a managerial position within the control of marine operations within a port.

IMarEST – Institute of Marine Engineering Science and Technology

www.imarest.org

IMarEST is the international professional body for all marine professionals, a registered charity and the first institute to bring together marine engineers, scientists and technologists into one international multi-disciplinary professional body.

IMO – International Maritime Organization

www.imo.org

The IMO is the United Nations' specialised agency with responsibility for the safety and security of shipping and the prevention of marine pollution by ships.

INTERCARGO – International Association of Dry Cargo Shipowners

www.intercargo.org

INTERCARGO members operate predominantly bulk carriers in the international dry bulk trades, such as coal, grain, iron ore and other bulk commodities. The Association's main role is to work with its members, regulators and other shipping associations to ensure that shipping operates safely, efficiently, environmentally and profitably.

INTERFERRY – International Ferry Owners' Association

www.interferry.com

INTERFERRY is the only shipping association representing the ferry industry worldwide. There are currently 225 members (representing approximately 600 individuals) from 38 countries.

INTERTANKO – International Association of Independent Tanker Owners

www.intertanko.com

INTERTANKO is a forum where the industry meets, policies are discussed and statements are created. It is a valuable source of first-hand information, opinions and guidance.

ISU – International Salvage Union

www.marine-salvage.com

The ISU is the global trade association representing marine salvors. Its members provide essential services to the world's maritime and insurance communities. Members are engaged in marine casualty response, pollution defence, wreck removal, cargo recovery, towage and related activities.

ITF – International Transport Workers' Federation

www.itfglobal.org

Around 700 unions, representing over 4.5 million transport workers from some 150 countries, are members of the ITF. It is one of several global union federations allied with the International Trade Union Confederation (ITUC).

ITOPF – International Tanker Owners Pollution Federation

www.itopf.co.uk

ITOPF is a not-for-profit organisation established on behalf of the world's shipowners to promote an effective response to marine spills of oil, chemicals and other hazardous substances.

MCA – Maritime and Coastguard Agency

www.dft.gov.uk/mca

The MCA implements the UK government's maritime safety policy in the United Kingdom and works to prevent the loss of life on the coast and at sea.

MPA – Maritime and Port Authority of Singapore

www.mpa.gov.sg

The Maritime and Port Authority of Singapore (MPA) was established on 2 February 1996, with the mission to develop Singapore as a global hub port and international maritime centre, and to advance and safeguard Singapore's strategic maritime interests.

NI – Nautical Institute

www.nautinst.org

The Nautical Institute is an international representative body for maritime professionals. It provides a wide range of services to enhance the professional standing and knowledge of its members who are drawn from all sectors of the maritime world.

OCIMF – Oil Companies International Maritime Forum

www.ocimf.com

OCIMF is a voluntary association of oil companies with an interest in the shipment and terminalling of crude oil, oil products, petrochemicals and gas.

RINA – Royal Institute of Naval Architects

www.rina.org.uk

RINA is an internationally-renowned professional institution whose members are involved at all levels in the design, construction, maintenance and operation of marine vessels and structures.

SIGTTO – Society of Gas Tanker and Terminal Operators

www.sigtto.org

SIGTTO was formed as an international organisation through which all industry participants might share experiences, address common problems and derive agreed criteria for best practices and acceptable standards.

SNAME – Society of Naval Architects and Marine Engineers

www.sname.org

SNAME has long been the pre-eminent society for practitioners of shipbuilding. It currently has an international membership of over 8,500 members.

US Environmental Protection Agency (EPA)

www.epa.gov

This is the agency responsible to the US Government for the administration of regulations concerning the protection of the environment. It works with the US Coast Guard on the enforcement of marine pollution regulations.

Marine fuels – technical and legal information

For detailed technical and legal information, I can recommend:

Bunkers: An Analysis of the Technical and Environmental Issues
Fourth edition. ISBN 978-1-908663-02-3. Chris Fisher and Robin Meech.
Published in 2013 by Petrospot Limited. www.petrospot.com/books

Bunkers: An Analysis of the Practical, Technical and Legal Issues
Third edition. ISBN 0-9548097-0-X. Chris Fisher and Jonathan Lux.
Published in 2004 by Petrospot Limited. www.petrospot.com/books

Legal Issues in Bunkering – An introduction to the law relating to the sale and use of marine fuels
First edition. ISBN 978-0-9548097-6-8. Trevor Harrison.
Published in 2011 by Petrospot Limited. www.petrospot.com/books

General

For general information on bunkering, I can recommend:

An Introduction to Bunkering
Second edition. ISBN 978-0-9548097-1-3. Nigel Draffin.
Published in 2012 by Petrospot Limited. www.petrospot.com/books

An Introduction to Fuel Analysis
First edition. ISBN 978-0-9548097-3-7. Nigel Draffin.
Published in 2009 by Petrospot Limited. www.petrospot.com/books

An Introduction to Bunker Operations
First edition. ISBN 978-0-9548097-4-4. Nigel Draffin.
Published in 2010 by Petrospot Limited. www.petrospot.com/books

An Introduction to Bunker Credit Risk
First Edition. ISBN 978-0-9548097-5-1. Adam Dupré.
Published in 2010 by Petrospot Limited. www.petrospot.com/books

Commercial Practice in Bunkering
First edition. ISBN 978-0-9548097-8-2. Nigel Draffin.
Published in 2011 by Petrospot Limited. www.petrospot.com/books

Bunker Fuel for Marine Engines
First Edition. ISBN 978-1-908663-00-9. Nigel Draffin.
Published in 2012 by Petrospot Limited. www.petrospot.com/books

Marine surveying

Report Writing for Marine Surveyors
First Edition. ISBN 978-0-9548097-7-5. Mike Wall.
Published in 2011 by Petrospot Limited. www.petrospot.com/books

Shipping law

Legal Issues in Bunkering
First Edition. ISBN 978-0-9548097-6-8. Trevor Harrison.
Published in 2011 by Petrospot Limited. www.petrospot.com/books

Essays in Admiralty
First Edition. ISBN 978-0-9548097-9-9. Jean Chiazor Anishere.
Published in 2012 by Petrospot Limited. www.petrospot.com/books

Appendix 2 - Ship sizes and dimensions

Ship type	Name	LOA m	Beam m	Laden draught m	Gross tonnage	Net tonnage	Capacity	Units
Oil tanker	Coastal tanker	103	18	6	4,599	1,958	6,000	tonne DWT
	Short sea	130	24	6	11,500	4,500	16,000	tonne DWT
	General purpose	180	30	11	24,000	9,000	35,000	tonne DWT
	Medium range	180	32	12.5	29,000	14,000	50,000	tonne DWT
	Long range 1	230	32	14	42,000	21,000	75,000	tonne DWT
	Long range 2	245	42	15.5	62,000	32,500	105,000	tonne DWT
	Suezmax	275	48	17	81,000	52,000	150,000	tonne DWT
	VLCC	340	56	20	160,000	95,000	300,000	tonne DWT
Gas tanker	LPG pressurised	95	15	5	4,000	1,200	3,500	cubic metre
	LPG semi refrigerated	150	25	10	16,750	5,050	23,000	cubic metre
	LPG fully refrigerated	225	35	12	47,000	18,000	80,000	cubic metre
	LNG	295	45	11	112,000	20,000	140,000	cubic metre
	LNG Q-flex	310	50	12	136,000	35,000	210,000	cubic metre
	LNG Q-max	345	54	12	164,000	51,500	265,000	cubic metre
Bulk Carrier	Coaster	77	15	4	1,600	900	3,500	tonne DWT
	Handy size	175	26	9	17,500	10,000	25,000	tonne DWT
	Handymax	185	32	12	30,000	18,000	55,000	tonne DWT

Category	Type							Unit
	Panamax	225	32	14	41,000	25,000	75,000	tonne DWT
	Capesize	290	45	18	87,000	55,000	175,000	tonne DWT
	Valemax	360	75	23	198,000	68,000	400,000	tonne DWT
Container	Small feeder	100	16	6	4,000	2,250	500	TEU
	Feeder	155	23	8	12,500	5,400	1,000	TEU
	Feedermax	215	32	10	34,000	14,200	2,250	TEU
	Panamax	290	32	12	53,000	33,000	4,900	TEU
	Post Panamax	335	42	12	94,000	38,000	9,000	TEU
	New Panamax	365	48	15	141,000	60,000	13,000	TEU
	ULCV	400	60	14.5	195,000	80,000	18,000	TEU
Passenger	River ferries	80	12	2	650		100	PAX
	Short sea ferries	180	28	6.5	25,000		1,000	PAX
	Specialist cruise ships	180	25	5	30,000		700	PAX
	Mid-size cruise ships	290	36	8	115,000		2,000	PAX
	Mega cruise ships	360	65	9.5	225,000		5,000	PAX
Car Carriers	Intermediate	155	27	8	28,000	8,366	3,000	CEU
	Large	195	32	9.5	59,000	18,000	6,000	CEU
	Very large	230	32	10	68,060	25,775	8,000	CEU
Warships	Patrol craft	50	8	2			350	displacement
	Corvette	85	12	3			1,000	displacement

	Frigate	125	15	4			3,600	dis-placement
	Destroyer	155	20	9			8,000	dis-placement
	Aircraft carrier	270	60	10			70,000	dis-placement
	Large aircraft carrier	335	80	12			100,000	dis-placement

Note - passenger ships do not normally have a net tonnage and warships are measured only by displacement.

Appendix 3 - Commercial agreements

Model voyage charter (extract)*

	CODE NAME: "Nigelvoy 4" Part I
1. Shipbroker	
	2. Place and date
3. Owners/Place of business (Cl. 1)	4. Charterers/Place of business (Cl. 1)
5. Vessel's name (Cl. 1)	6. GT/NT (Cl. 1)
7. DWT all told on summer load line in metric tons (abt.) (Cl. 1)	8. Present position (Cl. 1)
9. Expected ready to load (abt.) (Cl. 1)	
10. Loading port or place (Cl. 1)	11. Discharging port or place (Cl. 1)
12. Cargo (also state quantity and margin in Owners'option, it agreed; it tull and complete cargo not agreed state "part cargo") (Cl. 1)	
13. Freight rate (also state whether freight prepaid or payable on delivery) (Cl. 4)	14. Freight payment (state currency and method of payment; also beneficiary and bank account) (Cl. 4)
15. State if vessel's cargo handling gear shall not be used (Cl. 5)	16. Laytime (if separate laytime for load, and disch. is agreed, fill in a) and b). If total laytime for load, and disch., fill in c) only) (Cl. 6)
17. Shippers/Place of business (Cl. 6)	a) Laytime for loading
18. Agents (loading) (Cl. 6)	b) Laytime for discharging
19. Agents (discharging) (Cl. 6)	c) Total laytime for loading and discharging
20. Demurrage rate and manner payable (loading and discharging) (Cl. 7)	21. Cancelling date (Cl. 9)
	22. General Average to be adjusted at (Cl. 12)
23. Freight Tax (state if for the Owners' account) (Cl. 13 (c))	24. Brokerage commission and to whom payable (Cl. 1
25. Law and Arbitration (state 19 (a), 19 (b) or 19 (c) of Cl. 19; if 19 (c) agreed also state Place of Arbitration) (if not filled in 19 (a) shall apply) (Cl. 19) (a) State maximum amount for small claims/shortened arbitration (Cl. 19)	26. Additional clauses covering special provisions, if agreed
It is mutually agreed that this Contract shall be performed subject to the conditions contained in this Charter Party which shall include Part I as well as Part II. In the event of conflict of conditions, the provisions of Part I shall prevail over those of Part II to the extent of such conflict.	
Signature (Owners)	Signature (Charterers)

1. It is agreed between the party mentioned in Box 3 as the Owners of the Vessel 1

named in Box 5, of the GT/NT indicated in Box 6 and carrying about the number 2

of metric tons of deadweight capacity all told on summer loadline stated in Box 3

7, now in position as stated in Box 8 and expected ready to load under this 4

Charter Party about the date indicated in Box 9, and the party mentioned as the 5

Charterers in Box 4 that: 6

The said Vessel shall, as soon as her prior commitments have been completed, 7

proceed to the loading port(s) or place(s) stated in Box 10 or so near thereto as 8

she may safely get and lie always afloat, and there load a full and complete 9

cargo (if shipment of deck cargo agreed same to be at the Charterers' risk and 10

responsibility) as stated in Box 12, which the Charterers bind themselves to 11

ship, and being so loaded the Vessel shall proceed to the discharging port(s) or 12

place(s) stated in Box 11as ordered on signing Bills of Lading, or so near 13

thereto as she may safely get and lie always afloat, and there deliver the cargo. 14

2. Owners' Responsibility Clause 15

The Owners are to be responsible for loss of or damage to the goods or for 16

delay in delivery of the goods only in case the loss, damage or delay has been 17

caused by personal want of due diligence on the part of the Owners or their 18

Manager to make the Vessel in all respects seaworthy and to secure that she is 19

properly manned, equipped and supplied, or by the personal act or default of 20

the Owners or their Manager. 21

* This extract is for purposes of illustration only and should not be used as the basis for any commercial transaction.

Model time charter extract*

IT IS THIS DAY AGREED between_*Blue Chip Tankers*
Of _*Marshall Islands*___   (hereinafter referral to as "Owners"), being owners of the
good motor/steam vessel called_*Optimist*_ (hereinafter referred to as 'the vessel')
described as per Clause 1 hereof and *Fly By Night Chartering*_ of _*Monaco*__
(hereinafter referred to as "Charterers"):
1.   At the date of delivery of the vessel under this charter and throughout the charter
period:
(a)   she shall be classed by a Classification Society which is a member of the
International Association of Classification Societies;
(b)   she shall be in every way fit to carry crude petroleum and/or its products;
(c)   she shall be fit, staunch, strong, in good order and condition, and in every way fit
for the service, with her machinery, boilers, hull at other equipment (including but not
limited to hull stress calculator, radar, computers and computer systems) in a good and
efficient state;
(d)   her tanks, valves and pipelines shall be oil-tight,
(e)   she shall be in every way fitted for burning, in accordance with the grades
specified in clause 29 hereof:
         (i)   at sea, fuel oil for main propulsion and fuel oil/marine diesel for
         auxiliaries;
         (ii)   in port, fuel oil / marine diesel oil for auxiliaries;
(f)   she shall comply with regulations in force so as to enable her to pass though the
Suez and Panama Canals by day at night without delay,
(g)   she shall have on board all certificates, documents and equipment required from
time to time by any applicable law to enable her to perform the charter service without
delay;
(h)   she shall comply with the description in to OCIMF Harmonized Vessel Particulars
Questionnaire appended hereto as Appendix A, provided however that if there is any
conflict between the provisions of this questionnaire and any other provision, including
this Clause 1 of this charter such other provisions shall govern;
(i)   her ownership structure, flag, registry, classification society and management
company shall not be changed;
(j)   Owners will operate:
         (i)   a safety management system certified to comply with the International
         Safety Management code ("ISM code") for the Safe Operation of Ships and for
         Pollution Prevention;
         (ii)   a documented safe working procedures system (including procedures for
         the identification and mitigation of risks);
         (iii)   a documented environmental management system
         (iv)   documented accident / incident reporting system compliant with flag state
         requirements;
(k)   Owners shall submit to Charterers a monthly written report detailing all accidents /
incidents and environmental requirements, in accordance with the "FBN Safety and
Environmental Monthly Reporting Template" appended hereto as Appendix B;
(l)   Owners shall maintain Health Safety Environmental ("HSE") records sufficient to
demonstrate compliance with their HSE system and of this charter. Charterers reserve the
right to confirm compliance with HSE requirements by audit of owners.
(m)   Owners will arrange at their expense for a SIRE inspection to be carried out at
intervals of six months plus or minus thirty days.

2(a)   At the date of delivery of the vessel under this charter and throughout the charter period:

> (i)   she shall have a full and efficient compliment of master, officers and crew for a vessel of her tonnage, who shall in any event be not less than the number required by the laws of the flag state and who shall be trained to operate the vessel and her equipment competently and safely;
>
> (ii)   all shipboard personnel shall hold valid certificates of competence in accordance with the requirements of the law of the flag state;
>
> (iii)   all shipboard personnel shall be trained in accordance with the relevant provisions of the International Convention on Standards of Training, Certification and Watchkeeping for Seafarers (1995) or any additions, modifications or subsequent versions thereof;
>
> (iv)   there shall be on board sufficient personnel with a good working knowledge of the English language to enable cargo operations at loading and discharge places to be carried out efficiently and safely and to enable communications between the vessel and those loading the vessel or accepting discharge there from to be carried out quickly and efficiently;
>
> (v)   the terms of employment of the vessel's staff and crew will always remain acceptable to the International Transport Workers Federation and the vessel will at all times carry a Blue Card;
>
> (vi)   the nationality of the vessel's officers given in the OCIMF Vessel Particulars Questionnaire referred to in Clause 1(h) will not change without Charterers' prior agreement

(b) Owners guarantee that throughout the charter service the master shall with the vessel's officers and crew, unless otherwise ordered by charterers;

> (i)   prosecute all voyages with utmost dispatch;
>
> (ii)   render all customary assistance; and
>
> (iii)   load and discharge cargo as rapidly as possible when required by Charterers or their agents to do so, by night or by day, but always in accordance with the laws of the place of loading or discharging (as the case may be) and in each case in accordance with any applicable laws of the flag state.

3 (a) Throughout the charter service Owners shall, whenever passage of time, wear and tear or any event (whether or not coming within Clause 27 hereof) requires steps to be taken to maintain or restore the conditions stipulated in clauses 1 and 2(a), exercise due diligence so to maintain or restore the vessel.

(b) If at any time whilst the vessel is on hire under this charter the vessel fails to comply with the requirements of Clauses 1, 2(a) or 10 then hire shall be reduced to the extent necessary to indemnify Charterers for such failure. If and to the extent that such failure affects the time taken by the vessel to perform any services under this charter, hire shall be reduced by an amount equal in value, calculated at the rate of hire, of the time so lost. Any reduction of hire under this sub clause (b) shall be without prejudice to any other remedy available to charterers, but where such reduction of hire is in respect of time lost, such time shall be excluded from any calculation under Clause 24.

(c) If Owners are in breach of their obligations under Clause 3(a), Charterers may so notify in writing and if, after 30 days following receipt by Owners of any such notice, Owners have failed to demonstrate to Charterers' reasonable satisfaction the exercise of due diligence as required in Clause 3(a), the vessel shall be off-hire, no further hire payments shall be due, until Owners have so demonstrated that they are exercising such due diligence.

(d)   Owners shall advise Charterers immediately, in writing, should the vessel fail an inspection by, but not limited to, a governmental and or port state authority, and or terminal and or major charterer of similar tonnage. Owners shall simultaneously advise Charterers of their proposed course of action to remedy the defects which have caused the failure of such inspection.

(e)   If, in Charterers reasonably held view

    (i)   failure of an inspection, or,

    (ii)   any finding of an inspection, referred to in Clause 3(d),

prevents normal commercial operation then Charterers have the option to place the vessel off-hire from the date and time that the vessel fails such inspection, or becomes commercially inoperable, until the date and time that the vessel passes a re-inspection by the same organisation, or becomes commercially operable, which shall be in a position no less favourable to Charterers than at which she went off-hire.

(f)   Furthermore, at any time while the vessel is off-hire under this Clause 3 (with the exception of Clause 3 (e) (ii)), Charterers have the option to terminate the charter by giving notice in writing with effect from the date on which such notice of termination is received by Owners or from any later date stated in such notice. This sub-Cause (f) is without prejudice to any rights of Charterers or obligations of Owners under this charter or otherwise (including without limitation Charterers' rights ender Clause 21 hereof).

4. (a) Owners agree to let and Charterers agree to hire the vessel for a period of _3 years_ plus or minus _10_ days in Charterers' option commencing from the time and date of delivery of the vessel, for the purpose of carrying all lawful merchandise (subject always to Clause 28) including in particular _Fuel Oil_____;

in any part of the world, as Charterers shall direct, subject to the limits of the current British Institute Warranties and any subsequent amendments thereof. Notwithstanding the foregoing, but subject to Clause 35, Charterers may order the vessel to ice-bound waters or to any part of the world outside such limits provided that Owner's consent thereto (such consent not to be unreasonably withheld) and that Charterers pay for any insurance premium required by the vessel's underwriters as a consequence of such order.

(b) Any time during which the vessel is off-hire under this charter may be added to the charter period in Charterers option up to the total amount of time spent off-hire .In such cases the rate of hire will be that prevailing at the time the vessel would, but for the provisions of this clause, have been redelivered.

(c) Charterers shall use due diligence to ensure that the vessel is only employed between and at safe places (which expression when used in this charter shall include ports, berths, wharves, docks, anchorages, submarine lines, alongside vessels or lighters and other locations including locations at sea) where she can safely lie always afloat. Notwithstanding anything contained in this clause any other clause of this charter, Charterers do not warrant the safety of any place to which they order the vessel and shall be under no liability in respect thereof except for loss or damage causal by their failure to exercise due diligence as aforesaid. Subject as above, the vessel shall be loaded and discharged at any places as Charterers may direct, provided that Charterers shall exercise due diligence to ensure that any ship-to-ship transfer operations shall conform to standards not less than these set out in the latest published edition of the ICS/OCIMF Ship-to-Ship Transfer guide.

(d) Unless otherwise agreed, the vessel shall be delivered by Owners dropping outward pilot at a port in _Singapore_____

at Owners option and redelivered to Owners dropping outward pilot

at a port in __South East Asia_

at Charterers option.

(e) The vessel will deliver with last cargo(es) of _fuel oil__ and will redeliver with last cargo(es) of _fuel oil____

(f) Owners are required to give Charterers _30_ days prior notice of delivery and Charterers are
required to give Owners _30_ days prior notice of redelivery.
5. The vessel shall not be delivered to Charterers before 15th April 2014
Charterers shall have the option of cancelling this charter if the vessel is not ready and at their disposal on or before _1st May 2014__
6. Owners undertake to provide and to pay for all provisions, wages (including but not limited to all overtime payments), and shipping and discharging fees and all other expenses of the master, officers and crew, also, except as provided in Clauses 4 and 34 hereof, for all insurance on the vessel, for all deck, cabin and engine-room stores, and for water; for all drydocking, overhaul, maintenance and repairs to the vessel; and for all fumigation expenses and de-rat certificates. Owners' obligations under this Clause 6 extend to all liabilities for customs or import duties arising at any time during the performance of this charter in relation to the personal effect of the master, officers and crew, and in relation to the stores, provisions and other matters aforesaid which Owners are to provide and pay for and Owners shall refund to Charterers any sums Charterers or their agents may have paid or been compelled to pay in respect of any such liability. Any amounts allowable in general average for wages and provisions and stores shall be credited to Charterers insofar as such amounts were in respect of a period when the vessel is on-hire.
7. (a) Charterers shall provide and pay for all fuel (except fuel used for domestic services), towage and pilotage and shall pay agency fees, port charges, commissions, expenses of loading and unloading cargoes, canal dues and all charges other than those payable by Owners in accordance with Clause 6 hereof, provided that all charges for the said items shall be for Charterers' account when such items are consumed, employed or incurred for Owners' purposes or while the vessel is off-hire (unless such items reasonably relate to any service given or distance made good and taken into account under Clause 21 or 2; and provided further that any fuel used in connection with a general average sacrifice or expenditure shall be paid for by Owners.
(b) In respect of bunkers consumed for Owners' purposes these will be charged on each occasion by Charterers on a "first in – first out" basis valued on the price actually paid by Charterers.
(c) If the trading limits of this charter include ports in the United States of America and / or its protectorates then Charterers shall reimburse Owners for port specific charges relating to additional premiums charged by providers of oil pollution cover, when incurred by the vessel calling at ports in the United States of America and / or its protectorates in accordance with Charterers orders.
8. Subject as herein provided, Charterers shall pay for the use and hire of the vessel at the rate of United States Dollars 15,000.00__ day, and pro rata for any part of a day, from the time and date of her delivery (local time) to Charterers until the time and date of redelivery (local time) to Owners.
9. Subject to Clause 3(c) and 3(e), payment of hire shall be made in immediately available funds to _Blue Chip Tankers_____

_Optimist number 2 account_____

Account
__Cheerful Shipping Bank, Theadneedle Street, London, UK_____
__IBAN GB22 CSBK 6016 1331 9268 19_____
__SWIFT CSBKGB22 Acount number 31926819_____

 * This extract is for purposes of illustration only and should not be used as the basis for any commercial transaction.

Summary of INCOTERMS

Any mode of transport

The seven rules defined by Incoterms 2010 for any mode(s) of transportation are:

EXW – Ex Works (named place of delivery)

The seller makes the goods available at his/her premises. The buyer is responsible for uploading. This term places the maximum obligation on the buyer and minimum obligations on the seller. The Ex Works term is often used when making an initial quotation for the sale of goods without any costs included. EXW means that a seller has the goods ready for collection at his premises (works, factory, warehouse, plant) on the date agreed upon. The buyer pays all transportation costs and also bears the risks for bringing the goods to their final destination. The seller does not load the goods on collecting vehicles and doesn't clear them for export. If the seller does load the goods, he does so at buyer's risk and cost. If parties wish the seller to be responsible for the loading of the goods on departure and to bear the risk and all costs of such loading, this must be made clear by adding explicit wording to this effect in the contract of sale.

FCA – Free Carrier (named place of delivery)

The seller delivers goods, cleared for export, to the buyer-designated carrier at a named and defined location. This is used for any mode of transport. The seller must load goods onto the buyer's carrier. The key document signifying transfer of responsibility is receipt by carrier to exporter.

CPT – Carriage Paid To (named place of destination)

The seller pays for carriage. Risk transfers to buyer upon handling goods over to the first carrier at place of shipment in the country of export.

This term is used for all kind of shipments.

CIP – Carriage and Insurance Paid to (named place of destination)

The containerised transport/multimodal equivalent of CIF. Seller pays for carriage and insurance to the named destination point, but risk passes when the goods are handed over to the first carrier.

DAT – Delivered at Terminal (named terminal at port or place of destination)

Seller pays for carriage to the terminal, except for costs related to import clearance, and assumes all risks up to the point that the goods are unloaded at the terminal.

DAP – Delivered at Place (named place of destination)

Seller pays for carriage to the named place, except for costs related to import clearance, and assumes all risks prior to the point that the goods are ready for unloading by the buyer. Import clearance = import duty and VAT and not the Import Customs Clearance.

DDP – Delivered Duty Paid (named place of destination)

Seller is responsible for delivering the goods to the named place in the country of the buyer, and pays all costs in bringing the goods to the destination including import duties and taxes. The seller is not responsible for unloading. This term is often used in place of the non-Incoterm 'Free In Store (FIS)'. This term places the maximum obligations on the seller and minimum obligations on the buyer.

Sea and inland waterway transport

The four rules defined by Incoterms 2010 for international trade where transportation is entirely conducted by water are:

FAS – Free Alongside Ship (named port of shipment)

The seller must place the goods alongside the ship at the named port. The seller must clear the goods for export. Suitable only for maritime transport but *not* for multimodal sea transport in containers (see Incoterms 2010, ICC publication 715). This term is typically used for heavy-lift or bulk cargo.

FOB – Free onboard (named port of shipment)

The seller must load the goods onboard a vessel designated by the buyer. Cost and risk are divided when the goods are actually on board the vessel. The seller must clear the goods for export. The term is applicable for maritime and inland waterway transport only but *not* for multimodal sea transport in containers (see Incoterms 2010, ICC publication 715). The buyer must instruct the seller the details of the vessel and the port where the goods are to be loaded, and there is no reference to, or provision for, the use of a carrier or forwarder. This term has been greatly misused over the last three decades ever since Incoterms 1980 explained that FCA should be used for container shipments.

It means the seller pays for transportation of goods to the port of shipment, loading cost. The buyer pays cost of marine freight transportation, insurance, uploading and transportation cost from the arrival port to destination. The passing of risk occurs when the goods pass the ship's rail at port of shipments.

CFR – Cost and Freight (named port of destination)

Seller must pay the costs and freight to bring the goods to the port of destination. However, risk is transferred to the buyer once the goods are loaded on the vessel. Insurance for the goods is *not* included. This term is formerly known as CNF (C&F, or C+F). Maritime transport only.

CIF – Cost, Insurance and Freight (named port of destination)

Exactly the same as CFR except that the seller must in addition procure and pay for the insurance. Maritime transport only.

Incoterms 2010	Export-Customs declaration	Carriage to port of export	Unloading of truck in port of export	Loading charges in port of export	Carriage [Sea Freight/Air Freight] to port of import	Unloading charges in port of import	Insurance	Loading on truck in port of import	Carriage to place of destination	Import Customs clearance	Import taxes
EXW	Buyer	Buyer	Buyer	Buyer	Buyer	Buyer	Buyer	Buyer	Buyer	Buyer	Buyer
FCA	Seller	Seller	Buyer	Buyer	Buyer	Buyer	Buyer	Buyer	No	No	
FAS	Seller	Seller	Seller	Buyer	Buyer	Buyer	Buyer	Buyer	Buyer	Buyer	Buyer
FOB	Seller	Seller	Seller	Seller	Buyer	Buyer	Buyer	Buyer	Buyer	Buyer	Buyer
CPT	Seller	Seller	Seller	Seller	Seller	Buyer	Buyer	Buyer	Buyer	Buyer	Buyer
CFR	Seller	Seller	Seller	Seller	Seller	Buyer	Buyer	Buyer	Buyer	Buyer	Buyer
CIF [By Sea Only]	Seller	Seller	Seller	Seller	Seller	Buyer	Seller	Buyer	Buyer	Buyer	Buyer
CIP	Seller	Seller	Seller	Seller	Seller	Seller	Seller	Buyer	Buyer	Buyer	Buyer
DAT	Seller	Seller	Seller	Seller	Seller	Seller	Seller	Buyer	Buyer	Buyer	Buyer
DAP	Seller	Seller	Seller	Seller	Seller	Seller	Seller	Seller	Seller	Buyer	Buyer
DDP	Seller	Seller	Seller	Seller	Seller	Seller	Seller	Seller	Seller	Seller	Seller

Index